The
SOUP
Bible

pi

Publications International, Ltd.

Photography on pages 21, 31, 43, 47, 49, 55, 59, 63, 77, 79, 81, 83, 89, 97, 105, 113, 153, 161, 175 and 187 by PIL Photo Studio.
Photographer: Tate Hunt
Photographer's Assistant: Annemarie Zelasko
Prop Stylist: Tom Hamilton
Food Stylists: Kim Hartman, Walter Moeller
Assistant Food Stylists: Brittany Culver, Sheila Grannen, Lissa Levy

Pictured on the front cover *(top to bottom):* Bacon Potato Chowder *(page 22)* and Black Bean and Bacon Soup *(page 50)*.
Pictured on the back cover *(counterclockwise from top):* Ravioli Soup *(page 174)*, Sausage & Zucchini Soup *(page 160)* and Pumpkin Soup with Bacon and Toasted Pumpkin Seeds *(page 214)*.

ISBN-13: 978-1-4508-7558-5
ISBN-10: 1-4508-7558-0

Library of Congress Control Number: 2013937069

Manufactured in China.

8 7 6 5 4 3 2 1

Microwave Cooking: Microwave ovens vary in wattage. Use the cooking times as guidelines and check for doneness before adding more time.

Preparation/Cooking Times: Preparation times are based on the approximate amount of time required to assemble the recipe before cooking, baking, chilling or serving. These times include preparation steps such as measuring, chopping and mixing. The fact that some preparations and cooking can be done simultaneously is taken into account. Preparation of optional ingredients and serving suggestions is not included.

Publications International, Ltd.

contents

Introduction

Everyone loves soup! Soup is the satisfying mix of comfort and nourishment. It can be part of a meal or the whole meal. The magic of soup can start with leftovers in the refrigerator or a trip to the grocery store. Soup can be the hearty and healthy answer to a busy schedule; it is versatile, economical and easy to make.

The Soup Bible will guide you through the world of soup, from its history to the equipment you need to the garnishes that go on top. Learn how to make a variety of soups from this inspiring collection of more than 150 recipes.

History

Early records indicate that soup as we know it was consumed by ancient civilizations. Two things were needed to produce soup: a container to hold the ingredients and a way to heat them up. The containers were varied and creative: reptile or large mollusk shells, animal organs (especially stomachs), hollowed-out tree limbs and skin bags. Organs and skin bags might have had a stick through the top to suspend them over an open fire. Hollowed-out tree limbs and animal shells were simply placed on top of the fire.

The discovery of these cooking methods also led to a significant change in food intake for civilizations. Bones could now be used to make rich, nourishing broth. Roots, tubers and grains, previously tough and inedible, became tender, flavorful additions to the ancient diet after simmering in hot broth. This combination of meat with bones, vegetables and grains provided new flavors and tastes and enabled those with worn-down teeth to stay nourished with softer foods. Soups also contained less ash than food cooked directly on the fire.

Soup has been part of many cultures and cuisines throughout history. Ancient Romans reportedly served a fish broth and Greeks sold pea soup in the markets. Soups in Turkey contained many vegetables and were traditionally served throughout the day.

Historical records show that commoners in Europe cooked soup with local grains and a narrow assortment of ingredients. Upper classes used a wider variety of ingredients. Before the widespread use of the spoon in Europe around the fourteenth century, soup may have been served in one bowl on the table and shared by all. Large ingredients were pulled out by hand or with a knife.

In Medieval times, soup was simply liquid with some "sops" of bread or meat in it. A host who served soups with a great number of "sops" was considered generous. Travelers during this time carried something called "pocket soup," a firm piece of food made from concentrated stock similar to the modern bouillon cube. They would break off a small piece and add it to hot water to make soup. Pocket soup could keep for a long time, providing travelers with nourishment throughout their journey.

Soup as we know it became more prominent than "sops" around the seventeenth century. LaVarenne (author and chef who is credited with revolutionizing French cuisine) had recipes in his cookbook for stock and a French chef opened a restaurant that served soups exclusively. Another restaurant was opened in Boston by a chef nicknamed

"Prince of Soups." Soup recipes were included in both the first American cookbook printed in the early 1700s and another early American cookbook published in 1796.

Ingredients for soup during this time were varied. Vegetables included beet root, celery, carrots, squash and peas; seafood included crawfish and catfish; and meat could be beef, chicken, turkey, rabbit or turtle.

As you cook your way through The Soup Bible, think about the evolution of soup. It has fed, nourished and satisfied countless cultures across the world. It has developed through time as a source of basic nutrition and comfort. Remember that soups can be made with almost any meat, vegetable or grain. Experimenting with seasonings is encouraged. And there are only a few simple guidelines to follow. Enjoy!

Many cultures are known for a particular soup that reflects the identity of their cuisine. Here are some examples:

1. Minestrone (Italy)
2. Bouillabaisse (Provence)
3. Gazpacho (Spain)
4. Borscht (Russia)
5. Czarnina (Poland)
6. Avgolemono (Greece)

7. Melokhia (Egypt)
8. Peanut Soup (West Africa)
9. Bird's Nest Soup (China)
10. Black Bean Soup (Brazil)
11. Albondigas (Mexico)

1.   3.   6.   10.   11.

Souper Substitutions

Ingredient	Substitution
1 tablespoon fresh herbs	1 teaspoon dried herbs
Use about ⅓ of the dry amount when substituting for fresh herbs	
1 garlic clove	⅛ teaspoon garlic powder
2 tablespoons all-purpose flour	1 tablespoon cornstarch
1 cup broth	1 bouillon cube dissolved in 1 cup hot water
1 cup sour cream	1 cup plain yogurt
butter	olive oil
white rice	brown rice
shredded American cheese	shredded mild Cheddar cheese
white wine	reduced-sodium chicken broth

The Well-Stocked Soup Pantry

A well-stocked pantry can make preparing homemade soup quick and effortless. Consider keeping the following ingredients on hand.

Canned and Jarred Foods

1. Beans: Great Northern, chickpeas, kidney (red or white), black, pinto, navy, refried

2. Broth or bouillon cubes: chicken, beef, vegetable

3. Canned fish: salmon, tuna, clams, crabmeat

4. Canned condensed soup: tomato, green pea, cream of mushroom, nacho cheese, cream of potato, French onion, cream of celery

5. Chili sauce and/or ketchup

6. Evaporated milk

7. Green chiles (diced)

8. Oils: vegetable, canola, olive, sesame

9. Pitted green olives

10. Salsa, picante sauce, taco sauce

11. Solid-pack pumpkin

12. Soy sauce: regular, reduced-sodium

13. Tomato products: stewed tomatoes, whole tomatoes, tomato paste, pizza sauce, tomato sauce, diced tomatoes, tomato juice

14. Vegetables: green beans, corn (whole and cream-style), mixed vegetables, straw mushrooms, baby corn, sweet potatoes, hominy, pearl onions, marinated artichoke hearts

15. Vinegar: white, balsamic, red wine

Dry Foods

1. Barley: quick-cooking, pearl

2. Cornmeal

3. Cornstarch

4. Croutons

5. Dried split peas (green or yellow), lentils, dried baby lima beans

6. Dry bread crumbs

7. Flour

8. Noodles: egg, rice, Japanese udon

9. Pasta (variety of sizes)

10. Rice: brown, white, wild

11. Sugar: white, brown

2.　　　4.　　　5.　　　7.　　　9.

Seasonings

1. Bay leaves

2. Caraway seeds

3. Chile powder

4. Curry powder

5. Dried basil

6. Dried dill

7. Dried mint

8. Dried oregano

9. Dried rosemary

10. Dried thyme

11. Garlic: fresh, powder

12. Ground cinnamon

13. Ground coriander

14. Ground cumin

15. Ground ginger

16. Ground nutmeg

17. Ground sage

18. Paprika

19. Red pepper flakes

20. Salt and pepper

1.　　　2.　　　3.　　　4.　　　7.

11.　　　15.　　　17.　　　18.　　　19.

Essential Equipment

Making soup does not require a lot of special equipment. A few top-notch items are sufficient for most soup recipes. Good-quality cookware is worth the price; it will last many years through many recipes. Buy the best quality that your budget allows.

Dutch Oven or Saucepan

One of the most important pieces of equipment for making soup is the Dutch oven or saucepan. Designed to hold larger volumes of liquid, the Dutch oven is a large deep round pot with two handles and straight sides. The saucepan is a large pot with one handle and deep straight or slightly flared sides. These pots are used for soups and stews where boiling or simmering is required. Buy a heavy-gauge pot with a thick bottom for even cooking.

Measuring Cups and Spoons

There are two kinds of measuring cups: liquid measure and dry measure. Liquid measuring cups have a spout for easy pouring and are available in capacities from 1 cup to 1 gallon. They are necessary for accurately measuring liquid ingredients like broth, water or milk. Dry measuring cups are usually sold in sets of four: $\frac{1}{4}$ cup, $\frac{1}{3}$ cup, $\frac{1}{2}$ cup and 1 cup. A 2-cup measure is also available. They are used for measuring dry ingredients like vegetables, rice or chopped cooked meat.

Measuring spoons are usually sold in sets of four: $\frac{1}{4}$ teaspoon, $\frac{1}{2}$ teaspoon, 1 teaspoon and 1 tablespoon. These are most often used for measuring seasonings and spices like salt and pepper, as well as for measuring small amounts of liquids like vinegar.

Knives

High-quality sharp knives are absolutely essential in the kitchen. Every kitchen needs at least three knives: a paring knife, a utility knife and a chef's knife. Other knives can be purchased as the need arises. A sharpening steel is a good investment for keeping knives sharpened. Good cutlery should be washed by hand, as dishwashers are often too hot.

Peeler

A peeler is used for potatoes, carrots and any other vegetables that need to be peeled before slicing or chopping. A y-shaped peeler is ideal for tough-skinned vegetables like butternut squash.

Colander

Colanders can be used for washing, rinsing, draining and holding. Lined with cheesecloth, they can also be used for straining liquids.

Timer

This is helpful when cooking soups, as timing can be a factor in preventing overcooking.

Slotted Spoon

A slotted spoon is useful when removing large ingredients such as meat or vegetables from a liquid mixture.

Whisk

Whisks are used to incorporate air into eggs and also to ensure complete and smooth mixing of two ingredients like flour and water. Whisking helps to blend the two into a smooth paste.

Grater/Shredder

When a recipe calls for grated or shredded cheese, or a shredded vegetable, this tool is indispensable. Graters can be made of metal or plastic and will have various sizes of holes with very sharp edges to shred ingredients into small uniform pieces.

Soup How-To's

Avoid overcooked pasta or rice in soups:

Cook pasta or rice separately and add to soup before serving. Add a few extra minutes to the cooking time to heat through.

Correct oversalting:

Add some peeled potato slices to the soup. Simmer for 5 to 10 minutes. The potato will absorb some of the salt. Discard the potato before serving.

Cut vegetables for soup:

Vegetables should be cut into small, uniform pieces. They should be identifiable and fit on a spoon. Match the size of all the vegetables for a professional look to the soup.

Determine serving size:

If soup is an appetizer or part of a meal, serve about ¾ to 1 cup per person. If soup is the meal, serve about 1¼ to 1½ cups per person.

Freeze soup:

Cream soups and soups with cheese do not freeze well. Other soups, such as vegetable soup or chicken soup do freeze well. Pour cooled soup into a freezer container or resealable freezer food storage bag; seal well. Soup can be frozen for up to 3 months.

Soups containing rice or pasta can be frozen, but some of the liquid will be absorbed by the starch and there may be a change in texture.

Make an interesting soup bowl:

Cut a thin slice from the top of a round crusty roll. Scoop out some of the inside bread, leaving about ½ to 1 inch of shell. Pour in the soup. Serve immediately.

Cut a thin slice from the bottom of a small pumpkin or a small acorn squash so it sits flat. Cut a thin slice from the top of the pumpkin.

Scoop out some of the insides, leaving about ½ inch of pumpkin shell. Pour in the soup. Serve immediately. The pumpkin can be used raw or cooked.

Make croutons for garnish:

Use any kind of bread—white, sourdough, baguette, French, whole wheat, etc. Cut into cubes; toss with melted butter or olive oil. Toss with a small amount of dried herbs (such as thyme, oregano or sage) and/or grated Parmesan cheese. Spread in a single layer on a baking sheet. Bake at 350°F for about 15 minutes, stirring occasionally until lightly browned. Cool; store in a covered container.

Prevent curdling when adding milk or cream to a cream soup:

Heat the milk or cream separately in a small saucepan. Add some of the hot soup to the heated milk, then add all the mixture back into the soup.

Purée soup:

Hot soup can be puréed by using either an immersion blender, a standard blender or a food processor.

An immersion blender is used to blend or purée the soup in the pot it was made in. There is no need to transfer a hot liquid.

A standard blender or food processor can also be used to blend or purée a soup. The best way to do this is to transfer the hot soup in batches and purée small amounts at a time. Pour hot soup into the blender container, filling about half full. Allow some of the steam to escape while blending by removing the center cap from the top; place a clean towel over the hole to prevent spatter. Pour the soup into a serving bowl and repeat with the remaining hot soup.

Reduce the fat:

If a recipe calls for milk, use 2%, 1% or skim but the results may vary. If a recipe calls for half-and-half, substitute fat-free half-and-half.

Reduce the sodium:

The sodium can be reduced in some recipes with a few minor changes. In place of soy sauce, substitute reduced-sodium soy sauce. In place of chicken broth, substitute reduced-sodium chicken broth. Some canned beans, canned vegetables and canned tomatoes and tomato products are also available in reduced-sodium versions.

Reheat a soup made with sour cream, milk or cream:

Reheat the soup over medium heat, stirring often. To prevent curdling, do not let soup come to a boil. Do not microwave.

Skim fat from soup:

Refrigerate soup after cooking; fat will float to the top. Solidified fat can then be easily spooned off and discarded.

Or take a large spoon and spoon off fat from the surface; discard. Fat can also be removed using a fat-separating pitcher, a pitcher that has a spout near the bottom. The fat will float to the top so the broth without the fat is poured off from the bottom.

Speed up preparation:

Occasionally parts of soup recipes can be prepared ahead of time. For instance, in Hearty Beefy Beer Soup (page 20), the round steak, onion, carrots and celery can be prepared ahead of time. Refrigerate until ready to continue with the recipe.

Using frozen vegetables in place of fresh vegetables can also speed up cooking time. Frozen vegetables will cook faster than fresh.

Cooking Terms

Boil

To heat a liquid until bubbles break the surface.

Simmer

To heat a liquid until bubbles barely break the surface, or are present only around the edges.

Chop

To cut food into small, irregularly-shaped pieces, about ¼ inch in size.

Dice

To cut food into small, uniform pieces about ⅛ to ½ inch in size.

Mince

To cut food into very tiny, irregularly-shaped pieces (smaller than chopped).

Strain

To pour a liquid through the small holes of a strainer or the wire mesh of a sieve to remove lumps or unwanted particles. Liquid may also be strained through a cheesecloth-lined colander.

Stir-Fry

To cook bite-size pieces of meat and/or vegetables over high heat in a small amount of oil. Ingredients are stirred constantly to ensure even cooking and to prevent burning.

Brown

To cook food quickly until the surface of the ingredient is brown. This gives the food an appetizing appearance and adds flavor and aroma.

Garnishing Guide

Garnishes should enhance the flavor of the soup and add visual appeal. They can also add texture.

The garnish can either be a main ingredient or one that will complement the flavors and textures of the soup.

Small amounts of a garnish are all that is needed.

Garnishes should be added just before serving. This keeps the garnishes fresh and helps to prevent them from sinking. Or, put out small bowls of garnishes and let guests add their own.

Garnishing Thin or Clear Soups

1. Finely chopped fresh herbs such as thyme, basil or parsley

2. Finely grated fresh vegetables such as carrot or red onion

3. Very small amount of red pepper flakes

4. Chopped green onion

5. Finely chopped jalapeño peppers

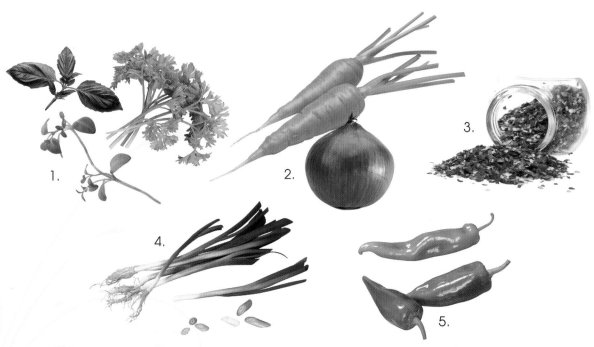

Garnishing Thicker Soups

1. Shredded cheese
2. Swirl or pattern of puréed vegetables
3. Toast cut into small shapes with cookie cutters
4. Pan-fried vegetable strips
5. Pan-fried garlic slices (thin slices of garlic cooked in a small amount of olive oil)
6. Swirl of prepared pesto
7. Chow mein noodles
8. Bacon bits
9. Bacon bits, chopped lettuce and chopped tomato for a BLT topping
10. Pretzels or shaped crackers
11. Crushed tortilla chips
12. Toasted sliced almonds
13. Toasted pecans
14. Salsa
15. Potato chips
16. Chopped hard-cooked eggs
17. Swirl of sour cream
18. Popcorn
19. Fresh herb leaves
20. Wedges of toasted pita bread
21. Croutons (store-bought or homemade)
22. Fresh vegetables cut into shapes with cookie cutters
23. Grated, shredded or shaved Parmesan cheese
24. Corn chips
25. Slices or pieces of the main vegetable ingredient
26. Thinly sliced sausage
27. Toasted French bread slices with melted cheese

1.
6.
7.
12.

15.
16.
18.
23.

Glossary

Bisque:

Bisque is a thick, rich cream soup made with shellfish or vegetables. Traditionally thickened with rice, flour is now often used. Bisques can either have pieces of chopped vegetables or shellfish, or be pureed.

Broth/Bouillon:

Broth is a thin, clear flavorful liquid made from simmering meats and or vegetables in water. Bouillon is the French word for broth and very often the terms are used interchangeably. Broth is usually the basis for soups and canned chicken, beef and vegetable broths are a great shortcut. Bouillon cubes and granules, made from dehydrated bouillon, are available in chicken, beef, vegetable and fish flavors. They need to be reconstituted with boiling water according to package directions. Since canned broth, bouillon cubes and granules tend to be salty, it is best to not add salt until the soup is finished cooking. Taste the soup and see if salt is needed.

Chowder:

Chowder is a thick, hearty soup made with fish, shellfish and occasionally vegetables. Chowders usually contain milk and potatoes.

Consommé:

Consommé is a thin, clear broth, concentrated for flavor and clarified to make it transparent. Egg whites and sometimes eggshells are added to broth and simmered for 10 to 15 minutes. The sediment in the broth becomes intertwined with the coagulated protein in the egg whites; the solidified proteins rise to the surface. The liquid is then strained through a cheesecloth-lined sieve. The resulting liquid is perfectly clear. Consommé can be eaten as is or used as a base for a soup recipe.

Cream Soup:

Cream soup is a thick, rich soup thickened with flour and has cream or milk added to it just before serving. The main flavoring ingredients can be strained out and discarded or puréed and added back to the soup.

Purée:

Purée soup is a thick soup with a coarser texture than a cream soup. It consists of a large amount of the main flavoring ingredient (meat, beans or vegetables) cooked in broth. Thickening is achieved by puréeing. Sometimes milk or cream is added at the end of cooking.

Stock:

Stock is the flavorful liquid resulting from the long simmering of meats, poultry, fish and/or bones in water. Vegetables such as onion, carrots, celery and leeks, in addition to herbs and spices, may be added. Stocks are the basis for soups. Because of the time needed to prepare stock, most soups today are made with prepared broth or bouillon.

beef
& pork

hearty beefy beer soup

  1 tablespoon vegetable oil

¾ pound round steak, cut into ½-inch cubes

  1 large onion, chopped

  2 medium carrots, sliced

  2 stalks celery, diced

  5 cups beef broth

  1 bottle (12 ounces) stout or dark ale

¾ teaspoon dried oregano

¼ teaspoon salt

⅛ teaspoon black pepper

  1 can (about 15 ounces) kidney beans, rinsed and drained

  1 small zucchini, cut into ½-inch cubes

  4 ounces mushrooms, sliced

1. Heat oil in Dutch oven or large saucepan over medium heat. Add beef, onion, carrots and celery. Cook and stir until meat is no longer pink and carrots and celery are crisp-tender.

2. Stir in broth, stout, oregano, salt and pepper. Bring to a boil over high heat. Reduce heat to low; simmer 45 minutes or until beef is fork-tender.

3. Stir beans, zucchini and mushrooms into soup. Bring to a boil over high heat. Reduce heat to low; simmer 5 minutes or until zucchini is tender. *Makes 6 servings*

hearty beefy beer soup

bacon potato chowder

4 slices bacon

1 large onion, chopped (about 1 cup)

4 cans (10¾ ounces each) CAMPBELL'S® Condensed Cream of Potato Soup

4 soup cans milk

¼ teaspoon ground black pepper

2 large russet potatoes, cut into ½-inch pieces (about 3 cups)

2 cups shredded Cheddar cheese (8 ounces)

½ cup chopped fresh chives

1. Cook bacon in a 6-quart saucepot over medium-high heat until it's crisp. Remove bacon with a fork and drain on paper towels. Crumble the bacon.

2. Add the onion and cook in the hot drippings until tender.

3. Stir the soup, milk, black pepper and potatoes into the saucepot. Heat to a boil. Reduce the heat to low. Cover and cook for 15 minutes or until the potatoes are tender. Remove from the heat.

4. Add the cheese and stir until the cheese melts. Serve with the chives.

Makes 8 servings

Transporting Tip: Transfer the chowder to a slow cooker. Chowder tends to thicken upon standing, so bring along some SWANSON® Vegetable or Chicken Broth to stir in before serving.

Prep Time: 15 minutes
Cook Time: 30 minutes

bacon potato chowder

ground beef, spinach and barley soup

¾ **pound ground beef**

 4 **cups water**

 1 **can (about 14 ounces) stewed tomatoes**

1½ **cups thinly sliced carrots**

 1 **cup chopped onion**

½ **cup quick-cooking barley**

1½ **teaspoons beef bouillon granules**

1½ **teaspoons dried thyme**

 1 **teaspoon dried oregano**

½ **teaspoon garlic powder**

¼ **teaspoon black pepper**

⅛ **teaspoon salt**

 3 **cups torn stemmed spinach**

1. Brown beef in large saucepan over medium-high heat 6 to 8 minutes, stirring to break up meat. Drain fat.

2. Stir in water, tomatoes, carrots, onion, barley, bouillon, thyme, oregano, garlic powder, pepper and salt. Bring to a boil over high heat.

3. Reduce heat to low; cover and simmer 12 to 15 minutes or until barley and vegetables are tender, stirring occasionally. Stir in spinach; cook until spinach starts to wilt.

Makes 4 servings

italian cupboard soup

 2 **boneless top loin pork chops, cubed**

 2 **(14½-ounce) cans chicken broth**

 1 **(15-ounce) can chopped tomatoes, undrained**

 1 **(15-ounce) can cannellini or great Northern beans, drained**

 2 **tablespoons dried minced onion**

 8 **ounces fresh spinach leaves, torn**

In deep saucepan, brown pork in small amount of oil; add chicken broth, tomatoes, beans and onion. Bring to a boil, lower heat and simmer for 15 minutes; stir in spinach and cook 2 minutes.

Top each serving with grated Parmesan or Romano cheese.

Makes 4 servings

Favorite recipe from **National Pork Board**

ground beef, spinach and barley soup

split pea soup

1 package (16 ounces) dried green or yellow split peas

7 cups water

1 pound smoked pork hocks *or* **4 ounces smoked sausage links, sliced and quartered**

2 medium carrots, chopped

1 medium onion, chopped

¾ teaspoon salt

½ teaspoon dried basil

¼ teaspoon dried oregano

¼ teaspoon black pepper

1. Rinse peas thoroughly in colander under cold running water; discard any debris or blemished peas.

2. Combine peas, water, pork, carrots, onion, salt, basil, oregano and pepper in Dutch oven or large saucepan. Bring to a boil over high heat. Reduce heat to low; simmer 1 hour and 15 minutes or until peas are tender, stirring occasionally. Stir frequently near end of cooking to keep soup from scorching.

3. Transfer pork to cutting board; cut into bite-size pieces. Place 3 cups soup in blender or food processor; blend until smooth.

4. Return puréed soup and pork to Dutch oven. If soup is too thick, add water until desired consistency is reached. Heat through. *Makes 6 servings*

 Tip | To purée soup, carefully pour the hot mixture into the blender. Cover with the lid, removing the center cap, then cover the hole with a towel. Start blending at low speed and gradually increase to high speed, blending to desired consistency.

split pea soup

kansas city steak soup

½ **pound ground beef**

3 **cups frozen mixed vegetables**

2 **cups water**

1 **can (about 14 ounces) stewed tomatoes**

1 **cup chopped onion**

1 **cup sliced celery**

1 **beef bouillon cube**

½ **to 1 teaspoon black pepper**

1 **can (about 14 ounces) reduced-sodium beef broth**

½ **cup all-purpose flour**

1. Brown beef in large saucepan over medium-high heat 6 to 8 minutes, stirring to break up meat. Drain fat.

2. Add mixed vegetables, water, tomatoes, onion, celery, bouillon cube and pepper to saucepan; bring to a boil.

3. Stir broth into flour in small bowl until smooth. Stir into soup until blended. Bring to a boil. Reduce heat to low; cover and simmer 15 minutes, stirring frequently.

Makes 6 servings

Note: If time permits, let the soup simmer an additional 30 minutes to allow the flavors to blend.

kansas city steak soup

kielbasa & cabbage soup

1 pound Polish kielbasa, cut into ½-inch cubes
1 package (16 ounces) coleslaw mix (shredded green cabbage and carrots)
3 cans (14½ ounces each) beef broth
1 can (12 ounces) beer or nonalcoholic malt beverage
1 cup water
½ teaspoon caraway seeds
2 cups *French's*® French Fried Onions, divided
Garnish: fresh dill sprigs (optional)

1. Coat 5-quart pot or Dutch oven with nonstick cooking spray. Cook kielbasa over medium-high heat about 5 minutes or until browned. Add coleslaw mix; sauté until tender.

2. Add broth, beer, water, caraway seeds and **1 cup** French Fried Onions; bring to a boil over medium-high heat. Reduce heat to low. Simmer, uncovered, 10 minutes to blend flavors. Spoon soup into serving bowls; top with remaining onions. Garnish with fresh dill sprigs, if desired.

Makes 8 servings

Prep Time: 10 minutes
Cook Time: 20 minutes

fiesta pork soup

1 pound lean ground pork
1 (14½-ounce) can chicken broth
1 (8-ounce) jar picante sauce
⅛ teaspoon ground cumin
⅛ teaspoon ground pepper
1 (11-ounce) can condensed fiesta nacho cheese soup
1 cup small round tortilla chips
¼ cup sour cream

In medium saucepan, cook and stir pork until browned. Drain. Add chicken broth, picante sauce, cumin and pepper; bring to a boil. Reduce heat; cover and simmer 15 minutes, stirring occasionally. Stir in cheese soup; simmer until heated through. Do not boil. Pour into serving bowls; garnish with tortillas chips and sour cream.

Makes 5 servings

Favorite recipe from **National Pork Board**

kielbasa & cabbage soup

hearty beef barley soup

Vegetable cooking spray

1 pound boneless beef sirloin or top round steak, cut into 1-inch cubes

2 cups sliced mushrooms

¼ teaspoon garlic powder

3½ cups SWANSON® Beef Broth (Regular, 50% Less Sodium or Certified Organic)

¼ teaspoon dried thyme leaves, crushed

Generous dash ground black pepper

2 medium carrots, sliced (about 1 cup)

½ cup uncooked quick-cooking barley

1. Spray a 6-quart saucepot with cooking spray. Heat over medium-high heat for 1 minute. Add the beef and cook until it's well browned and juices evaporate, stirring often.

2. Add the mushrooms and garlic powder to the saucepot. Cook until tender.

3. Add the broth, thyme, black pepper and carrots to the saucepot. Heat to a boil. Stir in the barley. Reduce the heat to low. Cover and cook over low heat 20 minutes or until the barley is done.   *Makes 4 servings*

Prep Time: 5 minutes
Cook Time: 30 minutes

oxtail soup with beer

2½ pounds oxtails (beef or veal)

1 large onion, sliced

4 carrots, cut into 1-inch pieces, divided

3 stalks celery, cut into 1-inch pieces, divided

2 sprigs fresh parsley

5 peppercorns

1 bay leaf

4 cups beef broth

8 ounces dark beer

2 cups diced baking potatoes

1 teaspoon salt

2 tablespoons chopped fresh parsley (optional)

continued on page 34

hearty beef barley soup

oxtail soup with beer, continued

1. Combine oxtails, onion, half of carrots, one third of celery, parsley, peppercorns and bay leaf in large saucepan; pour in broth and beer. Bring to a boil over high heat. Reduce heat to low; cover and simmer 3 hours or until meat is falling off bones.

2. Remove oxtails and set aside. Strain broth and return to saucepan; skim fat. Add remaining carrots, celery and potatoes; bring to a simmer. Cook 10 to 15 minutes or until vegetables are tender.

3. Remove meat from bones; return meat to saucepan. Stir in salt; heat through. Sprinkle each serving with chopped parsley, if desired. *Makes 4 servings*

sweet potato and ham soup

   1 tablespoon butter
   1 small leek, sliced
   1 clove garlic, minced
   4 cups reduced-sodium chicken broth
   2 medium sweet potatoes, peeled and cut into ¾-inch cubes
   ½ pound ham, cut into ½-inch cubes
   ½ teaspoon dried thyme
   2 ounces spinach, stemmed and torn

1. Melt butter in large saucepan over medium heat. Add leek and garlic. Cook and stir until leek is tender.

2. Add broth, sweet potatoes, ham and thyme to saucepan. Bring to a boil over high heat. Reduce heat to low; simmer 10 minutes or until sweet potatoes are tender.

3. Stir spinach into soup. Simmer 2 minutes or until spinach is wilted. Serve immediately.
Makes 6 servings

sweet potato and ham soup

zippy beef alphabet soup
with parmesan toasts

1 pound ground beef (95% lean)

½ teaspoon salt

¼ teaspoon pepper

2 cups water

1 can (14 to 14½ ounces) beef broth

1 can (15½ ounces) Great Northern beans, undrained

1 can (14½ ounces) Italian-style diced tomatoes, undrained

1 cup uncooked alphabet pasta

2 cups small broccoli florets

Salt and pepper

Grated or shredded Parmesan cheese (optional)

Parmesan Toasts

3 slices whole wheat bread

Olive oil for brushing

2 tablespoons grated or shredded Parmesan cheese

1. Heat oven to 350°F. Heat large nonstick skillet over medium heat until hot. Add ground beef; cook 8 to 10 minutes, breaking into ¾-inch crumbles and stirring occasionally. Season with ½ teaspoon salt and ¼ teaspoon pepper.

2. Add water, broth, beans, tomatoes and pasta; bring to a boil. Reduce heat; cover and simmer 5 minutes. Stir in broccoli; return to a boil. Reduce heat; cover and simmer 3 to 5 minutes or until broccoli is crisp-tender and pasta is tender. Season with salt and pepper, as desired.

3. Meanwhile prepare Parmesan Toasts. Cut out shapes from bread slices with cookie cutters. Place on baking sheet sprayed with nonstick cooking spray. Brush cutouts lightly with oil and sprinkle evenly with cheese. Bake in 350°F oven 6 to 8 minutes or until lightly toasted.

4. Serve soup with toasts; sprinkle with additional cheese, if desired.

Makes 4 servings

Cook's Tip: Cooking times are for fresh or thoroughly thawed ground beef. Ground beef should be cooked to an internal temperature of 160°F. Color is not a reliable indicator of ground beef doneness.

Prep and Cook Time: 25 to 30 minutes

Favorite recipe from **Courtesy The Beef Checkoff**

italian-style meatball soup

½ **pound ground beef**
¼ **pound bulk Italian sausage**
 1 **onion, finely chopped, divided**
⅓ **cup plain dry bread crumbs**
 1 **egg**
½ **teaspoon salt**
 4 **cups beef or vegetable broth**
 2 **cups water**
 1 **can (about 14 ounces) stewed tomatoes**
 1 **can (8 ounces) pizza sauce**
 2 **cups sliced cabbage**
 1 **can (about 15 ounces) kidney beans, rinsed and drained**
 2 **carrots, sliced**
½ **cup frozen Italian green beans**

1. Combine beef, sausage, 2 tablespoons onion, bread crumbs, egg and salt in large bowl; mix until well blended. Shape into 32 (1-inch) meatballs.

2. Brown half of meatballs in large skillet over medium heat, turning frequently. Remove from skillet; drain on paper towels. Repeat with remaining meatballs.

3. Bring broth, water, tomatoes and pizza sauce to a boil in Dutch oven or large saucepan over high heat. Add meatballs, remaining onion, cabbage, beans and carrots; bring to a boil. Reduce heat to low; simmer 20 minutes. Add green beans; simmer 10 minutes. *Makes 8 servings*

pork pozole

2 tablespoons vegetable oil

1 pound boneless pork loin, diced

1 large sweet onion, chopped (about 2 cups)

3 cloves garlic, minced

8 cups SWANSON® Chicken Broth (Regular, Natural Goodness® or Certified Organic)

1 teaspoon ground cumin

1 chipotle pepper in adobo sauce, minced

1 can (14½ ounces) diced tomatoes, undrained

1 can (15 ounces) hominy, rinsed and drained

¼ cup chopped fresh cilantro

1. Heat **1 tablespoon** of the oil in a 6-quart saucepot over medium-high heat. Add the pork and cook until it's well browned, stirring often. Remove the pork from the saucepot with a slotted spoon.

2. Add the remaining oil to the saucepot and reduce the heat to medium. Add the onion and garlic and cook until tender.

3. Stir in the broth, cumin, pepper, tomatoes and hominy. Heat to a boil. Return the pork to the saucepot and reduce the heat to low. Cover and cook for 35 minutes or until the pork is tender. Garnish with the cilantro. *Makes 6 servings*

Kitchen Tip: Hominy is dried white or yellow corn kernels with the germ and hull removed. When canned, it's ready to eat. Ground hominy is also known as corn grits or simply grits.

Prep Time: 15 minutes
Cook Time: 50 minutes

pork pozole

beefy broccoli & cheese soup

¼ **pound ground beef**

2 **cups beef broth**

1 **package (10 ounces) frozen chopped broccoli, thawed**

¼ **cup chopped onion**

1 **cup milk**

2 **tablespoons all-purpose flour**

1 **cup (4 ounces) shredded sharp Cheddar cheese**

1½ **teaspoons chopped fresh oregano** *or* ½ **teaspoon dried oregano**

Salt and black pepper

Hot pepper sauce

1. Brown beef in small nonstick skillet over medium-high heat 6 to 8 minutes, stirring to break up meat. Drain fat.

2. Bring broth to a boil in medium saucepan over high heat. Add broccoli and onion; cook 5 minutes or until broccoli is tender. Stir milk into flour in small bowl until smooth. Stir milk mixture and ground beef into saucepan; cook and stir until thickened and heated through.

3. Add cheese and oregano; stir until cheese is melted. Season with salt, black pepper and hot pepper sauce.

Makes 4 servings

beefy broccoli & cheese soup

harvest soup

½ pound **BOB EVANS® Special Seasonings Roll Sausage**
1 large onion, finely chopped
2½ cups chicken broth
2 cups canned pumpkin
2 cups hot milk
1 teaspoon lemon juice
Dash ground nutmeg
Dash ground cinnamon
Salt and black pepper to taste
Chopped fresh parsley

Crumble and cook sausage and onion in large saucepan until sausage is browned. Drain off any drippings. Add broth and bring to a boil. Stir in pumpkin; cover and simmer over low heat 15 to 20 minutes. Add milk, lemon juice, nutmeg, cinnamon, salt and pepper; simmer, uncovered, 5 minutes to blend flavors. Sprinkle with parsley before serving. Refrigerate leftovers. *Makes 6 to 8 servings*

 Tip | Canned pumpkin can be stored in a cool, dry place for up to 1 year. Refrigerate any open canned pumpkin in a tightly covered nonmetal container for up to 5 days.

harvest soup

veggie beef skillet soup

¾ **pound ground beef**

1 **tablespoon olive oil**

2 **cups coarsely chopped cabbage**

1 **cup chopped green bell pepper**

2 **cups water**

1 **can (about 14 ounces) stewed tomatoes**

1 **cup frozen mixed vegetables**

⅓ **cup ketchup**

1 **tablespoon beef bouillon granules**

2 **teaspoons Worcestershire sauce**

2 **teaspoons balsamic vinegar**

⅛ **teaspoon red pepper flakes**

¼ **cup chopped fresh parsley**

1. Brown beef in large skillet over medium-high heat 6 to 8 minutes, stirring to break up meat. Drain fat. Remove from skillet; set aside.

2. Heat oil in same skillet. Add cabbage and bell pepper; cook and stir 4 minutes or until cabbage is wilted. Add beef, water, tomatoes, mixed vegetables, ketchup, bouillon, Worcestershire sauce, vinegar and red pepper flakes; bring to a boil. Reduce heat; cover and simmer 20 minutes.

3. Remove from heat; let stand 5 minutes. Stir in parsley before serving.

Makes 4 servings

veggie beef skillet soup

long soup

1½ tablespoons vegetable oil

¼ small head cabbage, shredded

8 ounces boneless lean pork, cut into thin strips

6 cups chicken broth

2 tablespoons soy sauce

½ teaspoon minced fresh ginger

8 green onions, diagonally cut into ½-inch slices

4 ounces uncooked Chinese-style thin egg noodles

1. Heat oil in wok or large skillet over medium-high heat. Add cabbage and pork; cook and stir 5 minutes or until pork is no longer pink in center.

2. Add broth, soy sauce and ginger. Bring to a boil. Reduce heat to low; simmer 10 minutes, stirring occasionally. Stir in green onions.

3. Add noodles; cook 2 to 4 minutes or until noodles are tender.   *Makes 4 servings*

pork and noodle soup

1 package (1 ounce) dried shiitake mushrooms

4 ounces uncooked thin egg noodles

6 cups chicken broth

2 cloves garlic, minced

½ cup shredded carrots

4 ounces ham or Canadian bacon, cut into short thin strips

1 tablespoon hoisin sauce

⅛ teaspoon black pepper

2 tablespoons minced fresh chives

1. Place mushrooms in small bowl; cover with warm water. Soak 20 minutes to soften. Drain; squeeze out excess water. Discard stems; slice caps.

2. Meanwhile, cook egg noodles according to package directions until tender. Drain and set aside.

3. Combine broth and garlic in large saucepan. Bring to a boil over high heat; reduce heat to low. Add mushrooms, carrots, ham, hoisin sauce and pepper; simmer 15 minutes. Stir in noodles; simmer until heated through. Sprinkle with chives just before serving.   *Makes 6 servings*

long soup

vegetable beef noodle soup

½ **pound beef for stew, cut into ½-inch pieces**

¾ **cup unpeeled cubed potato (1 medium)**

½ **cup sliced carrot**

1 **tablespoon balsamic vinegar**

¾ **teaspoon dried thyme**

¼ **teaspoon black pepper**

2½ **cups reduced-sodium beef broth**

1 **cup water**

¼ **cup chili sauce or ketchup**

2 **ounces uncooked thin egg noodles**

¾ **cup jarred or canned pearl onions, rinsed and drained**

¼ **cup frozen peas**

1. Spray large saucepan with nonstick cooking spray. Heat over medium-high heat. Add beef; cook and stir 3 minutes or until browned on all sides. Remove from pan.

2. Add potato, carrot, vinegar, thyme and pepper to same saucepan; cook and stir 3 minutes over medium heat. Add broth, water and chili sauce. Bring to a boil over high heat; add beef. Reduce heat to low; cover and simmer 30 minutes or until meat is almost fork-tender.

3. Bring soup to a boil over high heat. Add noodles; cover and cook 7 to 10 minutes or until pasta is tender, stirring occasionally. Add onions and peas; heat 1 minute. Serve immediately. *Makes 6 servings*

vegetable beef noodle soup

black bean and bacon soup

5 strips bacon, sliced

1 medium onion, diced

2 tablespoons ORTEGA® Fire-Roasted Diced Green Chiles

2 cans (15 ounces each) ORTEGA® Black Beans, undrained

4 cups chicken broth

½ cup ORTEGA® Taco Sauce

½ cup sour cream

4 ORTEGA® Yellow Corn Taco Shells, crumbled

Cook bacon in large pot over medium heat 5 minutes or until crisp. Add onion and chiles. Cook 5 minutes or until onion begins to brown. Stir in beans, broth and taco sauce. Bring to a boil. Reduce heat to low. Simmer 20 minutes.

Purée half of soup in food processor until smooth (or use immersion blender in pot). Return puréed soup to pot and stir to combine. Serve with a dollop of sour cream and crumbled taco shells. *Makes 6 to 8 servings*

Note: For a less chunky soup, purée the entire batch and cook an additional 15 minutes.

Prep Time: 5 minutes
Start to Finish Time: 30 minutes

 Tip | Any unused bacon can be kept in the refrigerator for an additional 7 days. Keep the bacon in an airtight container, or wrap well in plastic wrap.

black bean and bacon soup

chicken & turkey

spaghetti soup

2 tablespoons vegetable oil

½ pound skinless, boneless chicken breast halves, cut into cubes

1 medium onion, chopped (about ½ cup)

1 large carrot, chopped (about ½ cup)

1 stalk celery, finely chopped (about ½ cup)

2 cloves garlic, minced

4 cups SWANSON® Chicken Broth (Regular, Natural Goodness® or Certified Organic)

1 can (10¾ ounces) CAMPBELL'S® Condensed Tomato Soup (Regular or Healthy Request®)

1 cup water

3 ounces uncooked spaghetti, broken into 1-inch pieces

2 tablespoons chopped fresh parsley (optional)

1. Heat **1 tablespoon** oil in a 6-quart saucepot over medium-high heat. Add the chicken and cook until it's well browned, stirring often. Remove the chicken from the saucepot.

2. Add the remaining oil to the saucepot and heat over medium heat. Add the onion and cook for 1 minute. Add the carrot and cook for 1 minute. Add the celery and garlic and cook for 1 minute.

3. Stir in the broth, soup and water. Heat to a boil. Stir in the pasta. Cook for 10 minutes or until the pasta is tender. Stir in the chicken and parsley, if desired, and cook until the mixture is hot and bubbling.

Makes 4 servings

Prep Time: 15 minutes
Cook Time: 30 minutes

spaghetti soup

turkey vegetable rice soup

1½ pounds turkey drumsticks (2 small)
8 cups cold water
1 medium onion, cut into quarters
2 tablespoons soy sauce
¼ teaspoon black pepper
1 bay leaf
2 medium carrots, peeled and sliced
⅓ cup uncooked rice
4 ounces mushrooms
1 cup fresh snow peas
1 cup coarsely chopped bok choy

1. Place turkey in Dutch oven or large saucepan. Add water, onion, soy sauce, pepper and bay leaf. Bring to a boil over high heat. Reduce heat to low; simmer, uncovered, 1½ hours or until turkey is tender.

2. Remove turkey from Dutch oven; let broth cool slightly. Skim fat; discard bay leaf.

3. Remove turkey meat from bones; discard skin and bones. Cut turkey into bite-size pieces.

4. Add carrots and rice to broth in Dutch oven. Bring to a boil over high heat. Reduce heat to low; simmer, uncovered, 10 minutes.

5. Meanwhile, wipe mushrooms clean with damp paper towel. Trim stems; cut mushrooms into slices.

6. Add mushrooms and turkey to soup. Bring to a boil over high heat. Reduce heat to low; simmer 5 minutes.

7. Cut snow peas in half crosswise. Stir snow peas and bok choy into soup. Bring to a boil over high heat. Reduce heat to low; simmer 8 minutes or until rice and vegetables are tender.

Makes 6 servings

turkey vegetable rice soup

spicy squash & chicken soup

1 tablespoon vegetable oil

1 small onion, finely chopped

1 stalk celery, finely chopped

2 cups cubed delicata or butternut squash (about 1 small)

2 cups chicken broth

1 can (about 14 ounces) diced tomatoes with chiles

1 cup chopped cooked chicken

½ teaspoon ground ginger

¼ teaspoon salt

⅛ teaspoon ground cumin

⅛ teaspoon black pepper

2 teaspoons lime juice

Fresh parsley or cilantro sprigs (optional)

1. Heat oil in large saucepan over medium heat. Add onion and celery; cook and stir 5 minutes or until crisp-tender. Stir in squash, broth, tomatoes, chicken, ginger, salt, cumin and pepper.

2. Cover and cook over low heat 30 minutes or until squash is tender. Stir in lime juice. Garnish with parsley.

Makes 4 servings

 Tip | Delicata and butternut are two types of winter squash. Delicata is an elongated, creamy yellow squash with green striations. Butternut is a long, light orange squash. Both have hard skins. To use, cut the squash lengthwise, scoop out the seeds, peel and cut into cubes.

spicy squash & chicken soup

southwest corn and turkey soup

2 dried ancho chiles* (each about 4 inches long) *or* **6 dried New Mexico chiles (each about 6 inches long)**

2 small zucchini

1 medium onion, thinly sliced

3 cloves garlic, minced

1 teaspoon ground cumin

3 cans (about 14 ounces each) reduced-sodium chicken broth

1½ to 2 cups (8 to 12 ounces) shredded cooked turkey

1 can (about 15 ounces) black beans or chickpeas, rinsed and drained

1 package (10 ounces) frozen corn

¼ cup cornmeal

1 teaspoon dried oregano

⅓ cup chopped fresh cilantro

*Ancho chiles can sting and irritate the skin, so wear rubber gloves when handling peppers and do not touch your eyes.

1. Cut stems from chiles; shake out seeds. Place chiles in medium bowl; cover with boiling water. Let stand 20 to 40 minutes or until chiles are soft; drain. Cut open lengthwise and lay flat on work surface. Scrape chile pulp from skin with edge of small knife. Finely mince pulp; set aside.

2. Cut zucchini in half lengthwise; cut crosswise into ½-inch slices.

3. Spray large saucepan with nonstick cooking spray; heat over medium heat. Add onion; cover and cook 3 to 4 minutes or until light golden brown, stirring occasionally. Add garlic and cumin; cook and stir about 30 seconds or until fragrant. Add broth, reserved chile pulp, zucchini, turkey, beans, corn, cornmeal and oregano; bring to a boil over high heat. Reduce heat to low; simmer 15 minutes or until zucchini is tender. Stir in cilantro. *Makes 6 servings*

southwest corn and turkey soup

green chile chicken soup
with tortilla dumplings

8 ORTEGA® Taco Shells, broken

½ **cup water**

⅓ **cup milk**

2 onions, diced, divided

1 egg

½ **teaspoon POLANER® Minced Garlic**

1 tablespoon olive oil

4 cups reduced-sodium chicken broth

2 cups shredded cooked chicken

2 tablespoons ORTEGA® Fire-Roasted Diced Green Chiles

¼ **cup vegetable oil**

Place taco shells, water, milk, **1 diced onion**, egg and garlic in blender or food processor. Pulse several times to crush taco shells and blend ingredients. Pour into medium bowl; let stand 10 minutes to thicken.

Heat olive oil in saucepan over medium heat. Add remaining diced onion; cook and stir 4 minutes or until translucent. Stir in broth, chicken and chiles. Reduce heat to a simmer.

Heat vegetable oil in small skillet over medium heat. Form taco shell mixture into 1-inch balls. Drop into hot oil in batches. Cook dumplings about 3 minutes or until browned. Turn over and continue cooking 3 minutes longer or until browned. Remove dumplings; drain on paper towels. Add dumplings to soup just before serving.

Makes 4 to 6 servings

Tip: For an even more authentic Mexican flavor, garnish the soup with fresh chopped cilantro and a squirt of lime juice.

Tip: For ease of preparation, purchase a cooked rotisserie chicken from your supermarket's hot deli case.

Prep Time: 15 minutes
Start to Finish Time: 30 minutes

green chile chicken soup with tortilla dumplings

chicken and homemade noodle soup

¾ **cup all-purpose flour**

2 **teaspoons finely chopped fresh thyme** *or* ½ **teaspoon dried thyme, divided**

¼ **teaspoon salt**

1 **egg yolk, beaten**

2 **cups plus 3 tablespoons cold water, divided**

1 **pound boneless skinless chicken thighs, cut into ½- to ¾-inch pieces**

5 **cups chicken broth**

1 **medium onion, chopped**

1 **medium carrot, thinly sliced**

¾ **cup frozen peas**

Chopped fresh parsley

1. For noodles, stir flour, 1 teaspoon thyme and salt in small bowl. Add egg yolk and 3 tablespoons water. Stir until well blended. Shape into small ball. Place dough on lightly floured surface; flatten slightly. Knead 5 minutes or until dough is smooth and elastic, adding more flour to prevent sticking if necessary. Cover with plastic wrap. Let stand 15 minutes.

2. Roll out dough to ⅛-inch thickness or thinner on lightly floured surface. If dough is too elastic, let rest several minutes. Let dough stand about 30 minutes to dry slightly. Cut into ¼-inch-wide strips. Cut strips 1½ to 2 inches long; set aside.

3. Combine chicken and remaining 2 cups water in medium saucepan. Bring to a boil over high heat. Reduce heat to low; cover and simmer 5 minutes or until chicken is cooked through. Drain chicken.

4. Combine broth, onion, carrot and remaining 1 teaspoon thyme in Dutch oven or large saucepan. Bring to a boil over high heat. Add noodles. Reduce heat to low; simmer 8 minutes or until noodles are tender. Stir in chicken and peas; heat through. Sprinkle with parsley.   *Makes 4 servings*

chicken and homemade noodle soup

turkey albondigas soup

½ **cup uncooked brown rice**

Meatballs

- **1 pound ground turkey**
- **2 tablespoons minced onion**
- **2 teaspoons chopped fresh cilantro**
- **2 teaspoons milk**
- **1 teaspoon hot pepper sauce**
- ¼ **teaspoon dried oregano**
- ¼ **teaspoon black pepper**

Broth

- **1 tablespoon olive oil**
- ¼ **cup chopped onion**
- **2 cloves garlic, minced**
- **5 cups reduced-sodium chicken broth**
- **1 tablespoon hot pepper sauce**
- **2 teaspoons tomato paste**
- ⅛ **teaspoon black pepper**
- **4 medium carrots, cut into rounds**
- **1 medium zucchini, quartered lengthwise and cut crosswise into ½-inch slices**
- **1 yellow squash, quartered lengthwise and cut crosswise into ½-inch slices**

Garnish

- **Lime wedges**
- **Fresh cilantro leaves**

1. Prepare rice according to package directions.

2. Meanwhile, lightly mix meatball ingredients in medium bowl until blended. Shape mixture into 1-inch balls.

3. For broth, heat oil in large saucepan over medium heat. Add onion and garlic; cook and stir until light golden brown. Add broth, hot pepper sauce, tomato paste and pepper. Bring to a boil over high heat. Reduce heat to low.

4. Add meatballs and carrots to broth mixture; simmer 15 minutes. Add zucchini, yellow squash and cooked rice. Simmer 5 to 10 minutes or until vegetables are tender.

5. Garnish with lime and cilantro.

Makes 4 to 6 servings

turkey albondigas soup

chicken and three-pepper corn chowder

12 *Tyson®* **Individually Frozen Boneless Skinless Chicken Tenderloins, thawed, cut into bite-size pieces**

2 tablespoons butter or margarine

3 cups frozen pepper and onion stir-fry mixture

1 large clove garlic, minced

2 cups frozen corn

1 cup chicken broth

⅛ teaspoon ground red pepper

2 cups (8 ounces) shredded or diced pasteurized process cheese product

½ cup whipping cream

1 tablespoon chopped fresh cilantro

4 cilantro sprigs (optional)

1. Wash hands. In large skillet, melt butter over medium heat. Add frozen vegetables; cook and stir 5 to 7 minutes or until tender. Add garlic; stir 30 seconds. Remove vegetables and set aside.

2. Add chicken tenders, corn, broth and red pepper to skillet; bring to a boil. Reduce heat; cover and simmer 5 minutes. Over medium heat, add cheese and cream to chicken mixture. Cook and stir until cheese is melted and internal juices of chicken run clear. (Or insert instant-read meat thermometer into thickest part of chicken. Temperature should read 180°F.) Stir in chopped cilantro.

3. Ladle into individual bowls. Garnish with cilantro sprigs. Refrigerate leftovers immediately. *Makes 4 servings*

Cook Time: 25 minutes

chicken and three-pepper corn chowder

turkey split-pea soup

Rich Turkey Stock (recipe follows) or 7 cups low-sodium chicken bouillon

1 pound dried split peas, washed and drained

2 cups chopped onions

1 cup chopped carrots

½ cup chopped celery

1 clove garlic, minced

3 tablespoons dried parsley

1 bay leaf

1 pound turkey ham, cut into ½-inch cubes

1. Prepare Rich Turkey Stock. In 5-quart saucepan, over high heat, combine stock, peas, onions, carrots, celery, garlic, parsley and bay leaf; bring to a boil. Reduce heat to simmer, cover and cook 1 hour. Remove saucepan from heat and discard bay leaf.

2. Whisk soup gently with wire whisk to blend peas. If desired, soup can be processed in food processor or blender for smoother texture.

3. Return soup to medium-high heat, add turkey ham and bring to a boil. Reduce heat to simmer and cook, uncovered, 10 to 15 minutes.   *Makes 8 servings*

Favorite recipe from **National Turkey Federation**

rich turkey stock

2 pounds bony turkey pieces (back, neck and wings)*

2 tablespoons vegetable oil

3 stalks celery with leaves, coarsely chopped

2 medium carrots, coarsely chopped

1 large onion, cut in chunks

1 to 4 cloves garlic (adjust amount used to taste), peeled

8 cups cold water

3 whole cloves

2 bay leaves

½ teaspoon dried thyme

1 teaspoon salt

¼ teaspoon whole black peppercorns

A leftover turkey carcass maybe substituted for turkey pieces.

1. Pat turkey pieces dry with clean paper towels.

2. Over medium-high heat, heat oil in a 5-quart saucepan or Dutch oven. In 2 to 3 batches, brown turkey pieces on all sides. Remove from pan with a slotted spoon and reserve in a large bowl.

3. Add celery, carrots, onion and garlic to pan and sauté until onion is tender, about 3 to 5 minutes.

4. Return turkey pieces to pan. Add water and bring mixture to a boil. Skim foam from surface.

5. Add remaining ingredients. Reduce heat, cover and simmer for 1 hour or until turkey pieces are tender.

6. Lift out turkey pieces with a slotted spoon. Strain stock through a sieve lined with 1 or 2 layers of cheesecloth. Discard vegetables, bay leaves and peppercorns.

7. Skim off fat. Use a metal spoon to ladle the fat off the top or chill stock and remove solidified fat layer.

8. When turkey is cool enough to handle, remove meat from bones. Discard skin and bones. Reserve meat for future use.

9. Stock may be used at once, stored in a closed container in the refrigerator 1 to 2 days, or stored in the freezer up to 6 months.

Favorite recipe from **National Turkey Federation**

 Tip | Turn this soup into a super supper. Buy small, round loaves of a hearty bread such as Italian or sourdough. Cut a small slice from the top and remove the inside bread, leaving about a 1-inch shell. Pour in soup and serve immediately.

easy chicken minestrone

4 *Tyson*® Trimmed & Ready™ Fresh Boneless Skinless Chicken Breasts
1 quart chicken broth
1 cup chopped onion
Salt, to taste
½ cup uncooked small pasta
1 package (10 ounces) frozen sliced carrots, thawed
2 cans (14½ ounces each) zucchini with Italian-style tomato sauce,* undrained

*Or substitute 1 can (14½ ounces) tomato sauce and 2 medium zucchini, cut in half and sliced.

1. Wash hands. Cut chicken into bite-size pieces. Wash hands.

2. Pour chicken broth into 2-quart stockpot. Bring to a boil over medium-high heat. Add chicken, onion and salt to taste. Cook over medium-high heat until chicken starts to turn white, about 5 minutes. Add pasta, carrots and zucchini. Cook 10 minutes more or until soup is heated thoroughly and internal juices of chicken run clear. (Or insert instant-read meat thermometer into thickest part of chicken. Temperature should read 180°F.)

3. Ladle into bowls and serve with focaccia bread, if desired. Refrigerate leftovers immediately. *Makes 4 servings*

Prep Time: 10 minutes
Cook Time: 15 minutes

 Tip | For a spicy flavor, add ½ teaspoon black pepper and ⅛ teaspoon ground red pepper or hot sauce to taste.

easy chicken minestrone

bounty soup

1 to 2 yellow squash (about ½ pound)

2 teaspoons vegetable oil

¾ pound boneless skinless chicken breasts, cut into ½-inch pieces

2 cups frozen mixed vegetables

1 teaspoon dried parsley flakes

⅛ teaspoon salt

⅛ teaspoon dried rosemary

⅛ teaspoon dried thyme

⅛ teaspoon black pepper

1 can (about 14 ounces) reduced-sodium chicken broth

1 can (about 14 ounces) stewed tomatoes

1. Cut wide part of squash in half lengthwise; lay flat and cut crosswise into ¼-inch-thick slices. Cut narrow part of squash into ¼-inch-thick slices.

2. Heat oil in large saucepan over medium-high heat. Add chicken; cook and stir 2 minutes. Stir in squash, mixed vegetables, parsley, salt, rosemary, thyme and pepper. Add broth and tomatoes, breaking large tomatoes apart. Bring to a boil. Reduce heat to low; cover and cook 5 minutes or until vegetables are tender and chicken is cooked through.   *Makes 4 servings*

Prep and Cook Time: 30 minutes

 | Yellow squash are also known as summer squash. They have thin, edible skins with a creamy white flesh. Because they are perishable, they should be stored in the refrigerator and used within 5 days of purchase.

bounty soup

turkey taco soup

  1 tablespoon olive oil
½ cup diced onions
  1 tablespoon POLANER® Minced Garlic
  1 pound ground turkey
  1 tablespoon ORTEGA® Chili Seasoning Mix
½ teaspoon salt
½ teaspoon black pepper
  3 cups chicken broth
  1 can (16 ounces) ORTEGA® Refried Beans
  1 tablespoon ORTEGA® Fire-Roasted Diced Green Chiles
  1 cup shredded lettuce
½ cup chopped tomato
  4 ORTEGA® Yellow Corn Taco Shells, crumbled

Heat oil in large saucepan over medium heat. Add onions and garlic; cook and stir 5 minutes. Stir in turkey, seasoning mix, salt and pepper. Cook and stir 5 minutes to break up turkey.

Add broth, beans and chiles; stir until beans are mixed in well. Cook over medium heat 10 minutes.

Divide soup among 6 bowls. Divide lettuce among bowls, and stir in to wilt lettuce slightly. Top each serving with chopped tomato and crumbled taco pieces.

Makes 6 servings

Tip: For additional flavor variations, use lean ground beef or ground chicken in this soup.

Prep Time: 5 minutes
Start to Finish Time: 30 minutes

turkey taco soup

chicken curry soup

6 ounces boneless skinless chicken breasts, cut into ½-inch pieces

3½ teaspoons curry powder, divided

1 teaspoon olive oil

¾ cup chopped apple

½ cup sliced carrot

⅓ cup sliced celery

¼ teaspoon ground cloves

2 cans (about 14 ounces each) reduced-sodium chicken broth

½ cup orange juice

4 ounces uncooked rotini pasta

Plain yogurt (optional)

1. Coat chicken with 3 teaspoons curry powder. Heat oil in large saucepan over medium heat. Add chicken; cook and stir 3 minutes or until cooked through. Remove from pan; keep warm.

2. Add apple, carrot, celery, remaining ½ teaspoon curry powder and cloves to same saucepan; cook 5 minutes, stirring occasionally. Add broth and orange juice; bring to a boil over high heat.

3. Reduce heat to low. Add pasta; cover and cook 8 to 10 minutes or until pasta is tender, stirring occasionally. Stir in chicken. Top each serving with dollop of yogurt, if desired. *Makes 4 servings*

chicken curry soup

skillet chicken soup

¾ **pound boneless skinless chicken breasts or thighs, cut into ¾-inch pieces**

1 **teaspoon paprika**

½ **teaspoon salt**

¼ **teaspoon black pepper**

2 **teaspoons vegetable oil**

1 **large onion, chopped**

1 **red bell pepper, cut into ½-inch pieces**

3 **cloves garlic, minced**

3 **cups reduced-sodium chicken broth**

1 **can (about 19 ounces) cannellini beans or small white beans, rinsed and drained**

3 **cups sliced savoy or napa cabbage**

½ **cup herb-flavored croutons, slightly crushed**

1. Toss chicken with paprika, salt and black pepper in medium bowl until coated.

2. Heat oil in large deep nonstick skillet over medium-high heat. Add chicken, onion, bell pepper and garlic. Cook and stir 5 minutes or until chicken is cooked through.

3. Add broth and beans; bring to a simmer. Cover and simmer 5 minutes. Stir in cabbage; cover and simmer 3 minutes or until cabbage is wilted. Top each serving with crushed croutons. *Makes 6 servings*

 Savoy cabbage, also called curly cabbage, is round with pale green crinkled leaves. Napa cabbage is also known as Chinese cabbage and is elongated with light green stalks.

skillet chicken soup

turkey noodle soup

2 (14½-ounce) cans chicken broth

1 cup water

2 tablespoons chopped fresh parsley

¼ teaspoon poultry seasoning

¼ teaspoon black pepper

2 cups cooked, cubed JENNIE-O TURKEY STORE® Oven Ready Homestyle Whole Turkey

1½ cups frozen mixed vegetables, thawed

4 ounces uncooked linguine or fettuccini

In large saucepan over medium-high heat, combine chicken broth, water, parsley, poultry seasoning and black pepper. Bring mixture to a boil. Add turkey, vegetables and pasta. Return to a boil. Reduce heat to low and cook for 8 to 10 minutes or until pasta is tender, stirring occasionally. *Makes 4 servings*

Prep Time: 15 minutes
Cook Time: 30 minutes

potato chicken soup

2½ pounds DOLE® Red Potatoes, peeled, cut into 1-inch cubes

½ pound DOLE® Mini Cut Carrots, halved

4 cups reduced-sodium chicken broth

½ bay leaf

2 teaspoons olive oil

1 small onion, cut into 1-inch cubes

1 teaspoon dried tarragon leaves, crushed

¼ teaspoon dried thyme leaves, crushed

1½ cups cooked diced chicken

1 to 2 tablespoons minced parsley

⅛ teaspoon salt

• Combine potatoes, carrots, chicken broth and bay leaf in large pot. Bring to boil; reduce heat and simmer 15 to 20 minutes.

• Heat oil in nonstick skillet. Add onion; cook 6 to 8 minutes or until lightly browned. Add tarragon and thyme; cook 30 seconds.

• Add onion mixture, chicken, parsley and salt to soup in pot. Cook 5 minutes longer or until heated through. Remove bay leaf before serving. *Makes 4 servings*

turkey noodle soup

chicken soup au pistou

½ **pound boneless skinless chicken breasts, cut into ½-inch pieces**

1 **large onion, diced**

3 **cans (about 14 ounces each) chicken broth**

1 **can (about 15 ounces) whole tomatoes, undrained**

1 **can (about 15 ounces) Great Northern beans, rinsed and drained**

2 **medium carrots, sliced**

1 **large potato, diced**

¼ **teaspoon salt**

¼ **teaspoon black pepper**

1 **cup fresh or frozen green beans, cut into 1-inch pieces**

¼ **cup prepared pesto**

Grated Parmesan cheese (optional)

1. Spray large saucepan with nonstick cooking spray; heat over medium-high heat. Add chicken; cook and stir 5 minutes or until chicken is browned. Add onion; cook and stir 2 minutes.

2. Add broth, tomatoes with juice, Great Northern beans, carrots, potato, salt and pepper. Bring to a boil, stirring to break up tomatoes. Reduce heat to low. Cover and simmer 15 minutes, stirring occasionally. Add green beans; cook 5 minutes or until vegetables are tender.

3. Top each serving with pesto; sprinkle with Parmesan cheese, if desired.

Makes 8 servings

chicken soup au pistou

chicken tortilla soup

1 teaspoon oil

1 clove garlic, minced

1 can (14½ ounces) chicken broth

1 jar (16 ounces) mild chunky-style salsa

¾ cup water

2 tablespoons *Frank's® RedHot®* Original Cayenne Pepper Sauce

1 package (10 ounces) fully cooked carved chicken breasts

1 can (8¾ ounces) whole kernel corn, undrained

1 tablespoon chopped fresh cilantro (optional)

1 cup crushed tortilla chips

½ cup (2 ounces) shredded Monterey Jack cheese

1. Heat oil in large saucepan over medium-high heat. Cook garlic 1 minute or until tender. Add broth, salsa, water and **Frank's RedHot** Sauce. Stir in chicken, corn and cilantro. Heat to boiling. Reduce heat to medium-low. Cook, covered, 5 minutes.

2. Stir in tortilla chips and cheese. Serve hot.   *Makes 4 servings*

cream of chicken and tortellini soup

½ (8-ounce) package dried tortellini

2 tablespoons butter

1 cup fresh snow peas, cut into 1-inch pieces

2 tablespoons all-purpose flour

3 cups chicken broth, heated

¼ cup half-and-half

1 cup diced cooked chicken breast

1 green onion, chopped

¼ cup grated Parmesan cheese (optional)

1. Cook tortellini according to package directions or until tender. Drain and set aside.

2. Meanwhile, melt butter in large saucepan over medium heat. Add snow peas; cook and stir 3 minutes or until crisp-tender. Stir in flour; cook and stir 1 minute. Pour in broth; cook and stir until mixture is slightly thickened. Stir in half-and-half, chicken, green onion and tortellini. Simmer 2 minutes or until pasta is heated through. Top each serving with Parmesan cheese, if desired.   *Makes 4 servings*

chicken tortilla soup

fish &
shellfish

new england fish chowder

¼ **pound bacon, diced**

 1 **cup chopped onion**

½ **cup chopped celery**

 2 **cups diced russet potatoes**

 2 **tablespoons all-purpose flour**

 2 **cups water**

 1 **bay leaf**

 1 **teaspoon salt**

 1 **teaspoon dried dill weed**

½ **teaspoon dried thyme**

½ **teaspoon black pepper**

 1 **pound cod, haddock or halibut fillets, skinned, boned and cut into 1-inch pieces**

 2 **cups milk or half-and-half**

   Chopped fresh parsley (optional)

1. Cook and stir bacon in Dutch oven over medium-high heat until crisp. Remove with slotted spoon; drain on paper towels. Add onion and celery to drippings. Cook and stir until onion is soft. Stir in potatoes; cook 1 minute. Stir in flour; cook 1 minute.

2. Add water, bay leaf, salt, dill, thyme and pepper. Bring to a boil over high heat. Reduce heat to low. Cover and simmer 25 minutes or until potatoes are fork-tender.

3. Add fish; cover and simmer 5 minutes or until fish begins to flake when tested with fork. Discard bay leaf. Add bacon and milk; heat through. *Do not boil.* Garnish with parsley.   *Makes 4 to 6 servings*

new england fish chowder

chick-pea and shrimp soup

1 tablespoon olive or vegetable oil

1 cup diced onion

2 cloves garlic, minced

4 cans (10½ ounces each) beef broth

1 can (14.5 ounces) CONTADINA® Recipe Ready Diced Tomatoes with Roasted Garlic, undrained

1 can (15 ounces) chick-peas or garbanzo beans, drained

1 can (6 ounces) CONTADINA® Italian Paste with Italian Seasonings

8 ounces small cooked shrimp

2 tablespoons chopped fresh Italian parsley or 2 teaspoons dried parsley flakes, crushed

½ teaspoon salt

¼ teaspoon ground black pepper

1. Heat oil over medium-high heat in large saucepan. Add onion and garlic; sauté for 1 minute.

2. Stir in broth, undrained tomatoes, chick-peas and tomato paste. Bring to boil.

3. Reduce heat to low; simmer, uncovered, 10 minutes. Add shrimp, parsley, salt and pepper; simmer 3 minutes or until heated through. Stir before serving.

Makes 8 to 10 servings

 Tip | Shrimp can be purchased in many forms from the grocery store: fresh, frozen, raw, cooked, shell-on or shelled. One pound of small raw shrimp will yield 8 ounces of cooked shrimp.

chick-pea and shrimp soup

scallops & mock seaweed soup

4 ounces spinach

3 carrots, peeled

6 cups chicken broth

4 green onions, sliced

2 tablespoons chopped fresh dill

2 teaspoons white wine Worcestershire sauce

2 teaspoons lemon juice

1 pound bay scallops, rinsed and patted dry

Salt and white pepper to taste

1. To cut spinach into thin strips, make V-shaped cut at stem end. Roll up and cut crosswise into ½-inch-thick slices.

2. To cut carrots decoratively, use citrus stripper or grapefruit spoon to make lengthwise grooves into carrots about ¼ inch apart. Thinly slice crosswise.

3. Bring broth to a simmer in large saucepan; add carrot slices. Bring to a boil. Reduce heat; simmer 5 minutes or until carrots are crisp-tender.

4. Add spinach, green onions, dill, Worcestershire sauce and lemon juice; simmer 2 minutes. Add scallops; simmer just until scallops turn opaque. Season with salt and pepper; serve immediately.

Makes 6 servings

scallops & mock seaweed soup

oyster stew

1 quart shucked oysters, with their liquor

8 cups milk

8 tablespoons margarine or butter, cut into pieces

1 teaspoon freshly ground white pepper

½ teaspoon salt

Paprika

2 tablespoons finely chopped fresh parsley

Heat oysters in their liquor in medium saucepan over high heat until oyster edges begin to curl, about 2 to 3 minutes. Heat milk and margarine together in large saucepan over medium-high heat just to boiling. Add pepper and salt.

Stir in oysters and their liquor. Do not boil or overcook stew or oysters may become tough. Pour stew into tureen. Dust with paprika; sprinkle with parsley.

Makes 8 servings

Favorite recipe from **National Fisheries Institute**

shrimp & corn chowder with sun-dried tomatoes

1 can (10¾ ounces) CAMPBELL'S® Condensed Cream of Potato Soup

1½ cups half-and-half

2 cups whole kernel corn

2 tablespoons sun-dried tomatoes, cut in strips

1 cup small or medium cooked shrimp

2 tablespoons chopped fresh chives

Ground black or ground red pepper

1. Heat the soup, half-and-half, corn and tomatoes in a 2-quart saucepan over medium heat to a boil. Cover and reduce the heat to low. Cook for 10 minutes.

2. Stir in the shrimp and chives and heat through.

3. Season to taste with black pepper.

Makes 4 servings

Kitchen Tip: For a lighter version, substitute skim milk for the half-and-half.

Prep Time: 5 minutes
Cook Time: 20 minutes

oyster stew

mediterranean fish soup

4 ounces uncooked small penne, pastina or other small pasta

¾ cup chopped onion

2 cloves garlic, minced

1 teaspoon whole fennel seeds

1 can (about 14 ounces) stewed tomatoes

1 can (about 14 ounces) reduced-sodium chicken broth

1 tablespoon minced fresh Italian parsley

½ teaspoon black pepper

¼ teaspoon ground turmeric

8 ounces firm, white-fleshed fish, cut into 1-inch pieces

3 ounces small raw shrimp, peeled with tails intact

1. Cook pasta according to package directions. Drain; set aside.

2. Meanwhile, spray large nonstick saucepan with nonstick cooking spray; heat over medium heat. Add onion, garlic and fennel seeds; cook and stir 3 minutes or until onion is tender.

3. Stir in tomatoes, broth, parsley, pepper and turmeric. Bring to a boil; reduce heat and simmer 10 minutes. Add fish; cook 1 minute. Add shrimp; cook until shrimp are pink and opaque. Divide pasta among 4 bowls; ladle soup over pasta.

Makes 4 servings

cranky crab bisque

¾ pound lump crabmeat or 2 (6-ounce) cans crabmeat

⅓ cup dry sherry

1 (11-ounce) can tomato soup, undiluted

1 (11-ounce) can green pea soup, undiluted

1 teaspoon Original TABASCO® brand Pepper Sauce

2 cups milk

Combine crabmeat and sherry in medium bowl; marinate 15 minutes. Heat soups and TABASCO® Sauce in 3-quart saucepan over low heat. Stir in milk until well blended and mixture is heated through. Just before serving, stir in crabmeat mixture; cook until heated through.

Makes 6 servings

mediterranean fish soup

manhattan clam chowder

¼ **cup chopped bacon**

1 **cup chopped onion**

½ **cup chopped carrots**

½ **cup chopped celery**

2 **cans (14.5 ounces each) CONTADINA® Recipe Ready Diced Tomatoes, undrained**

1 **can (8 ounces) CONTADINA® Tomato Sauce**

1 **bottle (8 ounces) clam juice**

1 **large bay leaf**

½ **teaspoon chopped fresh rosemary**

⅛ **teaspoon black pepper**

2 **cans (6½ ounces each) chopped clams, undrained**

1. Sauté bacon with onion, carrots and celery in large saucepan.

2. Stir in undrained tomatoes with remaining ingredients, except clams. Heat to boiling. Reduce heat; boil gently 15 minutes. Stir in clams and juice.

3. Heat additional 5 minutes. Remove bay leaf before serving.   *Makes 6½ cups*

Microwave Directions: Combine bacon, onion, carrots and celery in 2-quart microwave-safe casserole dish. Microwave on HIGH (100%) power 5 minutes. Stir in remaining ingredients, except clams. Microwave on HIGH (100%) power 5 minutes. Stir in clams and juice. Microwave on HIGH (100%) power 5 minutes. Remove bay leaf before serving.

manhattan clam chowder

savory seafood soup

2½ cups water or chicken broth
1½ cups dry white wine
1 onion, chopped
½ red bell pepper, chopped
½ green bell pepper, chopped
1 clove garlic, minced
½ pound halibut, cut into 1-inch chunks
½ pound sea scallops, cut into halves
1 teaspoon dried thyme
Juice of ½ lime
Dash hot pepper sauce
Salt and black pepper

1. Combine water, wine, onion, bell peppers and garlic in large saucepan; bring to a boil. Reduce heat to low. Cover and simmer 15 minutes or until bell peppers are tender, stirring occasionally.

2. Add fish, scallops and thyme; cook 2 minutes or until fish and scallops are opaque. Stir in lime juice and hot pepper sauce. Season with salt and black pepper; serve immediately.   *Makes 4 servings*

 Tip | Halibut is considered a lean fish because it has a low fat content. If halibut is not available, cod, ocean perch or haddock can be substituted. When buying fresh fish, store it tightly wrapped in the refrigerator and plan on using it within 2 days of purchase.

savory seafood soup

simply special seafood chowder

1 tablespoon olive or vegetable oil

1 medium bulb fennel, trimmed, cut in half and thinly sliced (about 2 cups)

1 medium onion, chopped (about ½ cup)

1 teaspoon dried thyme leaves, crushed

5 cups water

1¾ cups SWANSON® Vegetable Broth (Regular or Certified Organic)

1 can (10¾ ounces) CAMPBELL'S® Condensed Tomato Soup (Regular or Healthy Request®)

1 package (10 ounces) frozen baby whole carrots, thawed (about 1½ cups)

½ pound fresh or thawed frozen firm white fish fillets (cod, haddock or halibut), cut into 2-inch pieces

½ pound fresh large shrimp, shelled and deveined

¾ pound mussels (about 12), well scrubbed

Freshly ground black pepper

1. Heat the oil in a 4-quart saucepot over medium heat. Add the fennel, onion and thyme and cook until the vegetables are tender. Stir in the water, broth, soup and carrots and heat to a boil.

2. Stir in the fish. Cook for 2 minutes. Stir in the shrimp and mussels. Cover and reduce the heat to low. Cook for 3 minutes or until the fish flakes easily when tested with a fork, the shrimp turn pink and the mussels open. Discard any mussels that do not open.

3. Serve the soup with black pepper.   *Makes 6 servings*

Prep Time: 10 minutes
Cook Time: 20 minutes

simply special seafood chowder

corn and crab gazpacho

1 cucumber, peeled, seeded and coarsely chopped

3 green onions, coarsely chopped

2 tablespoons coarsely chopped fresh Italian parsley or cilantro

2 pounds grape or cherry tomatoes

3 cups tomato juice, chilled

1 cup cooked fresh corn (1 large ear) or thawed frozen corn

3 tablespoons olive oil

2 tablespoons red wine vinegar

1¼ teaspoons red pepper flakes

1 teaspoon salt

¼ teaspoon black pepper

1½ cups flaked cooked crabmeat (about 8 ounces) *or* 8 ounces cooked baby shrimp

1. Combine cucumber, green onions and parsley in food processor. Process using on/off pulsing action until finely chopped. Transfer to large bowl. Add tomatoes to food processor. Process using on/off pulsing action until finely chopped. Add to cucumber mixture.

2. Stir in tomato juice, corn, oil, vinegar, red pepper flakes, salt and black pepper. Cover and refrigerate 1 to 3 hours.

3. Top each serving with ¼ cup crabmeat.   *Makes 6 servings*

Variation: For a vegetarian version, omit crab.

Note: Gazpacho can be made several hours in advance and chilled. Bring to room temperature before serving.

cioppino

2 tablespoons olive or vegetable oil

1½ cups chopped onions

1 cup chopped celery

½ cup chopped green bell pepper

1 clove garlic, minced

1 can (28 ounces) CONTADINA® Recipe Ready Original Crushed Tomatoes

1 can (6 ounces) CONTADINA® Tomato Paste

1 teaspoon Italian herb seasoning

1 teaspoon salt

½ teaspoon ground black pepper

2 cups water

1 cup dry red wine or chicken broth

3 pounds clams, oysters, cooked crab, cooked lobster, whitefish, scallops and/or shrimp (in any proportion)

1. Heat oil in large saucepan. Add onions, celery, bell pepper and garlic; sauté until vegetables are tender. Add tomatoes, tomato paste, Italian seasoning, salt, black pepper, water and wine.

2. Bring to a boil. Reduce heat to low; simmer, uncovered, for 15 minutes.

3. To prepare fish and seafood, scrub clams and oysters under running water. Place in ½ inch boiling water in separate large saucepan; cover. Bring to a boil. Reduce heat to low; simmer just until shells open, about 3 minutes. Set aside.

4. Cut crab, lobster, fish and scallops into bite-size pieces. Shell and devein shrimp.

5. Add fish to tomato mixture; simmer 5 minutes. Add scallops and shrimp; simmer 5 minutes.

6. Add crab, lobster and reserved clams and oysters; simmer until heated through.

Makes about 14 cups

Prep Time: 30 minutes
Cook Time: 35 minutes

tortilla soup with grouper

   1 tablespoon vegetable oil

   1 onion, chopped

   2 cloves garlic, minced

3½ cups chicken broth

1½ cups tomato juice

   1 cup chopped tomatoes

   1 can (4 ounces) diced green chiles, drained

   2 teaspoons Worcestershire sauce

   1 teaspoon ground cumin

   1 teaspoon chili powder

   1 teaspoon salt

  ⅛ teaspoon black pepper

   3 corn tortillas, cut into 1-inch strips

   1 cup corn

   1 pound grouper fillets, cut into 1-inch cubes

1. Heat oil in large saucepan over medium-high heat. Add onion and garlic; cook and stir until softened. Stir in broth, tomato juice, tomatoes, chiles, Worcestershire sauce, cumin, chili powder, salt and pepper; bring to a boil. Reduce heat to low; cover and simmer 10 minutes.

2. Add tortillas and corn; cover and simmer 8 to 10 minutes.

3. Stir in fish. Simmer, uncovered, until fish begins to flake when tested with fork. Serve immediately. *Makes 6 servings*

tortilla soup with grouper

asian pasta & shrimp soup

1 package (3½ ounces) fresh shiitake mushrooms

2 teaspoons Asian sesame oil

2 cans (14½ ounces each) vegetable broth

4 ounces angel hair pasta, broken into 2-inch lengths (about 1 cup)

½ pound medium shrimp, peeled and deveined

4 ounces snow peas, cut into thin strips

2 tablespoons *French's*® Honey Dijon Mustard

1 tablespoon *Frank's*® *RedHot*® Original Cayenne Pepper Sauce

⅛ teaspoon ground ginger

1. Remove and discard stems from mushrooms. Cut mushrooms into thin strips. Heat oil in large saucepan over medium-high heat. Add mushrooms; stir-fry 3 minutes or just until tender.

2. Add broth and ½ cup water to saucepan. Heat to boiling. Stir in pasta. Cook 2 minutes or just until tender.

3. Add remaining ingredients, stirring frequently. Heat to boiling. Reduce heat to medium-low. Cook 2 minutes or until shrimp turn pink and peas are tender.

Makes 4 servings

Prep Time: 10 minutes
Cook Time: about 10 minutes

 Tip | To devein shrimp, cut a shallow slit along the back of the shrimp with a paring knife and lift out the vein. This may be easier to do under cold running water.

asian pasta & shrimp soup

tomato-basil crab bisque

1 tablespoon butter

½ cup chopped onion

1 can (8 ounces) HUNT'S® Tomato Sauce with Roasted Garlic

1 cup half-and-half

1 cup coarsely chopped cooked crabmeat

½ cup chicken broth

¼ teaspoon salt

⅛ teaspoon ground black pepper

¼ cup chopped fresh basil leaves

1. Melt butter in a medium saucepan over medium-high heat. Add onion; cook 3 minutes or until tender, stirring frequently.

2. Add tomato sauce, half-and-half, crab, broth, salt and pepper. Bring just to a boil; reduce heat to low. Cover tightly and simmer 5 minutes. Sprinkle with basil before serving.   *Makes 4 servings*

west coast bouillabaisse

1 cup sliced onion

2 stalks celery, cut diagonally into slices

2 cloves garlic, minced

1 tablespoon vegetable oil

4 cups chicken broth

1 can (28 ounces) tomatoes with juice, cut up

1 can (6½ ounces) minced clams with juice

½ cup dry white wine

1 teaspoon Worcestershire sauce

½ teaspoon dried thyme, crushed

¼ teaspoon bottled hot pepper sauce

1 bay leaf

1 cup frozen cooked bay shrimp, thawed

1 (6.4-ounce) STARKIST Flavor Fresh Pouch® Tuna (Albacore or Chunk Light)

Salt and pepper to taste

6 slices lemon

6 slices French bread

continued on page 110

tomato-basil crab bisque

In Dutch oven sauté onion, celery and garlic in oil for 3 minutes. Stir in broth, tomatoes with juice, clams with juice, wine, Worcestershire, thyme, hot pepper sauce and bay leaf. Bring to a boil; reduce heat. Simmer for 15 minutes. Stir in shrimp and tuna; cook for 2 minutes to heat. Remove bay leaf. Season with salt and pepper. Garnish with lemon slices and serve with bread. *Makes 6 servings*

cajun shrimp and potato chowder

1 tablespoon olive oil
½ pound medium shrimp (26 to 30 count), peeled, deveined (thawed if frozen)
½ cup chopped onion
½ cup chopped green bell pepper
2 cups SIMPLY POTATOES® Homestyle Slices, chopped slightly
1 can (14 ounces) chicken broth
2 teaspoons Cajun seasoning
2 tablespoons all-purpose flour
2 tablespoons water
1 can (14½ ounces) diced tomatoes, undrained

1. Heat oil in 2-quart saucepan over medium heat. Add shrimp, onion and green pepper. Cook, stirring occasionally, until shrimp is no longer pink. Add **Simply Potatoes®**, broth and Cajun seasoning. Bring to a boil. Reduce heat to low. Cook, stirring occasionally, until **Simply Potatoes®** are tender (20 to 25 minutes).

2. In small bowl, combine flour and water; stir until smooth. Add flour mixture to soup. Stir in tomatoes. Cook until soup is thickened and heated through.

Makes 4 servings

Total Time: 35 minutes

cajun shrimp and potato chowder

shrimp bisque

1 pound medium shrimp, peeled and deveined

½ cup chopped onion

½ cup chopped celery

½ cup chopped carrot

2 tablespoons butter or margarine

2 cans (14 ounces each) chicken broth

1 can (14½ ounces) DEL MONTE® Original Recipe Stewed Tomatoes, undrained

¼ teaspoon dried thyme

1 cup half-and-half

1. Cut shrimp into small pieces; set aside. In large saucepan, cook onion, celery and carrot in butter until onion is tender.

2. Add shrimp; cook 1 minute. Add broth, tomatoes and thyme; simmer 10 minutes. Ladle ⅓ of soup into blender container or food processor.

3. Cover and blend until smooth. Repeat with remaining soup. Return to saucepan. Add half-and-half. Heat through. *Do not boil.* Garnish with chopped parsley, if desired.

Makes 6 servings

Variation: Substitute 2 cans (6 ounces each) of crab for shrimp.

Prep Time: 15 minutes
Cook Time: 20 minutes

 Tip | Shrimp are available in various sizes: colossal, jumbo, extra-large, large, medium, small and extra small (also called baby or miniature). One pound of medium shrimp will contain about 31 to 35 shrimp.

shrimp bisque

salmon, corn & barley chowder

1 teaspoon canola oil

¼ cup chopped onion

1 clove garlic, minced

2½ cups reduced-sodium chicken broth

¼ cup quick-cooking barley

1 tablespoon water

1 tablespoon all-purpose flour

1 can (about 4 ounces) salmon, drained

1 cup frozen corn, thawed

⅓ cup milk

½ teaspoon chili powder

¼ teaspoon ground cumin

¼ teaspoon dried oregano

⅛ teaspoon salt

1 tablespoon minced fresh cilantro

⅛ teaspoon black pepper

Lime wedges (optional)

1. Heat oil in medium saucepan over medium heat. Add onion and garlic. Cook and stir 1 to 2 minutes or until onion is tender.

2. Add broth; bring to a boil. Stir in barley. Reduce heat to low; cover and simmer 10 minutes or until barley is tender.

3. Stir water into flour in small bowl until smooth; set aside. Remove and discard bones and skin from salmon; flake into bite-size pieces.

4. Add salmon, corn and milk to saucepan; stir until blended. Stir in flour mixture, chili powder, cumin, oregano and salt. Simmer 2 to 3 minutes or until slightly thickened. Stir in cilantro and pepper. Serve with lime wedges, if desired.   *Makes 2 servings*

salmon, corn & barley chowder

vegetables & beans

curried vegetable rice soup

1 package (16 ounces) frozen stir-fry vegetables
1 can (about 14 ounces) vegetable broth
¾ cup uncooked instant brown rice
2 teaspoons curry powder
½ teaspoon salt
½ teaspoon hot pepper sauce
1 can (14 ounces) unsweetened coconut milk
1 tablespoon lime juice

1. Combine vegetables and broth in large saucepan. Cover and bring to a boil over high heat. Stir in rice, curry powder, salt and hot pepper sauce. Reduce heat to low; cover and simmer 8 minutes or until rice is tender, stirring once.

2. Stir in coconut milk; cook 3 minutes or until heated through. Remove from heat; stir in lime juice. *Makes 4 servings*

Tip: For a lighter soup with less fat and fewer calories, substitute light unsweetened coconut milk. Most large supermarkets carry this in their international foods section.

Prep and Cook Time: 15 minutes

curried vegetable rice soup

white bean and escarole soup

1½ **cups dried baby lima beans**
1 **teaspoon olive oil**
½ **cup chopped celery**
⅓ **cup coarsely chopped onion**
2 **cloves garlic, minced**
2 **cans (about 14 ounces each) whole tomatoes, undrained, chopped**
½ **cup chopped fresh parsley**
2 **tablespoons chopped fresh rosemary**
¼ **teaspoon black pepper**
3 **cups shredded escarole**

1. Place lima beans in large glass bowl; cover completely with water. Soak 6 to 8 hours or overnight. Drain beans; place in large saucepan. Cover beans with about 3 cups water. Bring to a boil over high heat. Reduce heat to low; cover and simmer about 1 hour or until soft. Drain; return to saucepan and keep warm.

2. Heat oil in small skillet over medium heat. Add celery, onion and garlic; cook and stir 5 minutes or until onion is tender.

3. Add celery mixture and tomatoes with juice to beans. Stir in parsley, rosemary and pepper. Cover and simmer over low heat 15 minutes. Add escarole; simmer 5 minutes.

Makes 6 servings

 Tip | Store dried lima beans (also known as butter beans) in an airtight container in a cool, dry place for up to 1 year. When soaking, do not allow beans to soak for longer than 12 hours or they may start to ferment.

white bean and escarole soup

roasted red pepper salsa soup

2 tablespoons olive oil

1 onion, diced

½ teaspoon POLANER® Chopped Garlic

3 cups chicken broth

2 jars (12 ounces each) roasted red peppers, drained

1 cup ORTEGA® Original Salsa (Medium)

½ teaspoon salt

¼ cup canola oil

4 ORTEGA® Soft Flour Tortillas, cut into ¼-inch strips

1 teaspoon ORTEGA® Chili Seasoning Mix

Heat olive oil in large pot over medium heat until hot. Add onion and garlic. Cook and stir 3 minutes. Stir in broth, red peppers and salsa; bring to a boil. Reduce heat to low.

Purée soup in blender or food processor in batches until smooth (or use immersion blender in pot). Return puréed soup to pot. Add salt; stir to combine.

Heat canola oil in medium skillet over medium-high heat until hot. Drop tortilla strips into oil, several at a time. Carefully turn over when strips begin to brown. Remove from oil and drain on paper towel. Sprinkle strips with seasoning mix. Garnish soup with tortilla strips.   *Makes 6 servings*

Prep Time: 5 minutes
Start to Finish Time: 20 minutes

roasted red pepper salsa soup

potato soup with caramelized fig relish

1½ pounds white potatoes, cut into 1-inch pieces (about 5 cups)

1½ pounds sweet potatoes, cut into 1-inch pieces

3 tablespoons olive oil

Ground black pepper

8 cups SWANSON® Vegetable Broth (Regular or Certified Organic)

1 teaspoon ground sage

2 large shallots, finely chopped (about ½ cup)

1 cup dried mission figs, chopped

¼ cup sweet wine (white port, late harvest Riesling) or additional vegetable broth

1. Heat the oven to 425°F. Arrange the potatoes in a 17×11-inch roasting pan and toss with **2 tablespoons** of the oil. Season with black pepper. Bake for 25 minutes or until the potatoes are tender.

2. Purée the potato mixture and 1½ cups broth in batches until almost smooth. Pour the puréed mixture into a 3-quart saucepan. Stir in the remaining broth and sage. Cook over high heat to a boil. Reduce the heat to low. Cook for 10 minutes.

3. Meanwhile, in an 8-inch skillet, heat the remaining olive oil over medium-high heat. Add the shallots and cook for 4 minutes or until golden. Add the figs and wine and cook for 4 minutes more or until the liquid is absorbed and the figs are soft.

4. Divide the soup among **8** serving bowls and top **each** serving of soup with about **1 tablespoon** of the fig mixture.   *Makes 8 servings*

Prep Time: 10 minutes
Bake Time: 25 minutes
Cook Time: 25 minutes

potato soup with caramelized fig relish

ravioli minestrone

1 package (7 ounces) refrigerated 3-cheese ravioli
2 teaspoons olive oil
1 medium onion, chopped
2 carrots, chopped
1 stalk celery, chopped
2 cloves garlic, minced
6 cups water
1 can (about 15 ounces) chickpeas, rinsed and drained
1 can (about 14 ounces) diced tomatoes
3 tablespoons tomato paste
1 teaspoon dried basil
1 teaspoon dried oregano
¾ teaspoon salt
¾ teaspoon black pepper
1 medium zucchini, cut in half lengthwise and sliced (about 2 cups)
1 package (10 ounces) baby spinach

1. Cook ravioli according to package directions. Drain; keep warm.

2. Meanwhile, heat oil in Dutch oven or large saucepan over medium-high heat. Add onion, carrots, celery and garlic; cook and stir about 5 minutes or until vegetables are softened.

3. Stir in water, chickpeas, tomatoes, tomato paste, basil, oregano, salt and pepper. Bring to a boil; reduce heat and simmer 15 minutes or until vegetables are tender. Add zucchini; cook 5 minutes. Stir in spinach; cook 2 minutes or until spinach wilts. Stir in ravioli.

Makes 8 servings

Prep Time: 20 minutes
Cook Time: 27 minutes

ravioli minestrone

cuban-style black bean soup

2 teaspoons olive oil

1 small onion, chopped

1 cup thinly sliced carrots

2 jalapeño peppers,* seeded and minced

2 cloves garlic, minced

1 can (about 15 ounces) no-salt-added black beans, undrained

1 can (about 14 ounces) vegetable or chicken broth

¼ cup chopped fresh cilantro

¼ cup sour cream (optional)

4 lime wedges (optional)

*Jalapeño peppers can sting and irritate the skin, so wear rubber gloves when handling peppers and do not touch your eyes.

1. Heat oil in large saucepan over medium heat. Add onion, carrots, jalapeños and garlic; cook and stir 5 minutes.

2. Add beans and broth; bring to a boil. Reduce heat to low; cover and simmer 15 to 20 minutes or until vegetables are very tender.

3. Sprinkle each serving with cilantro. Serve with sour cream and lime wedges, if desired.   *Makes 4 servings*

Note: For a smooth, creamy soup, purée soup in batches in a food processor or blender.

cuban-style black bean soup

butternut squash soup

2 teaspoons olive oil

1 large sweet onion, chopped

1 medium red bell pepper, chopped

2 packages (12 ounces each) frozen butternut squash, thawed

1 can (10¾ ounces) condensed reduced-sodium chicken broth, undiluted

¼ teaspoon ground nutmeg

⅛ teaspoon white pepper

½ cup half-and-half

1. Heat oil in large saucepan over medium-high heat. Add onion and bell pepper; cook and stir 5 minutes. Add squash, broth, nutmeg and white pepper; bring to a boil over high heat. Reduce heat; cover and simmer 15 minutes or until vegetables are very tender. Purée soup in saucepan with hand-held immersion blender. Or transfer soup in batches to food processor or blender; process until smooth. Return soup to saucepan.

2. Stir in half-and-half; heat through. Swirl in additional half-and-half, if desired.

Makes 4 servings

santa fe tomato chowder

1 tablespoon butter or margarine

2 teaspoons minced garlic

4 ripe tomatoes, chopped

1 can (15 ounces) tomato sauce

1 cup frozen corn kernels

¼ cup chopped fresh cilantro

1 tablespoon *Frank's® RedHot®* Original Cayenne Pepper Sauce

½ teaspoon chili powder

1 ripe avocado, peeled and chopped

1 cup (4 ounces) shredded Monterey Jack cheese

1⅓ cups *French's®* French Fried Onions

1. Melt butter in large saucepan; sauté garlic for 1 minute. Add tomatoes and cook 5 minutes. Stir in 1 cup water, tomato sauce, corn, cilantro, **Frank's RedHot** Sauce and chili powder.

2. Bring to a boil over high heat. Reduce heat; simmer 10 minutes. Spoon soup into serving bowls; sprinkle with avocado, cheese and French Fried Onions.

Makes 4 servings

butternut squash soup

deep bayou chowder

       1 tablespoon olive oil
  1½ cups chopped onions
       1 large green bell pepper, chopped
       1 large carrot, chopped
       8 ounces red potatoes, diced
       1 cup frozen corn
       1 cup water
      ½ teaspoon dried thyme
       2 cups milk
       2 tablespoons chopped parsley
  1½ teaspoons seafood seasoning
      ¾ teaspoon salt

Heat oil in large saucepan over medium-high heat. Add onions, bell pepper and carrot; cook and stir 5 minutes. Add potatoes, corn, water and thyme; bring to a boil. Reduce heat; cover and simmer 15 minutes or until potatoes are tender. Stir in milk, parsley, seasoning and salt. Cook 5 minutes.   *Makes 6 servings*

mushroom barley soup

       1 tablespoon olive oil
       2 cups chopped onions
       1 cup thinly sliced carrots
       2 cans (about 14 ounces each) reduced-sodium vegetable broth
     12 ounces sliced mushrooms
       1 can (10¾ ounces) cream of mushroom soup, undiluted
      ½ cup uncooked quick-cooking barley
       1 teaspoon Worcestershire sauce
      ½ teaspoon dried thyme
      ¼ cup finely chopped green onions
      ¼ teaspoon salt
      ¼ teaspoon black pepper

Heat oil in large saucepan over medium-high heat. Add onions; cook and stir 8 minutes or until onions just begin to turn golden. Add carrots; cook and stir 2 minutes. Add broth, mushrooms, soup, barley, Worcestershire sauce and thyme; bring to a boil. Reduce heat; cover and simmer 15 minutes, stirring occasionally. Stir in green onions, salt and pepper.   *Makes 4 servings*

deep bayou chowder

sweet potato bisque

1 pound sweet potatoes, peeled and cut into 2-inch chunks
2 teaspoons butter
½ cup finely chopped onion
1 teaspoon curry powder
½ teaspoon ground coriander
¼ teaspoon salt
⅔ cup unsweetened apple juice
1 cup buttermilk
¼ cup water
Fresh snipped chives (optional)
Plain yogurt (optional)

1. Place potatoes in large saucepan; cover with water. Bring to a boil over high heat. Cook 15 minutes or until potatoes are fork-tender. Drain; cool under cold running water.

2. Meanwhile, melt butter in small saucepan over medium heat. Add onion; cook and stir 2 minutes. Stir in curry powder, coriander and salt; cook and stir about 1 minute or until onion is tender. Remove from heat; stir in apple juice.

3. Combine potatoes, buttermilk and onion mixture in food processor or blender; process until smooth. Pour mixture back into large saucepan; stir in ¼ cup water, if needed, to thin to desired consistency. (If soup is still too thick, add additional 1 to 2 tablespoons water.) Cook and stir over medium heat until heated through. *Do not boil.* Garnish with chives or yogurt.　　　　　　　　*Makes 4 servings*

sweet potato bisque

vegetable soup

2 tablespoons FILIPPO BERIO® Extra Virgin Olive Oil

2 medium potatoes, peeled and quartered

2 medium onions, sliced

3 cups beef broth

8 ounces fresh green beans, trimmed and cut into 1-inch pieces

3 carrots, peeled and chopped

8 ounces fresh spinach, washed, drained, stemmed and chopped

1 green bell pepper, diced

2 tablespoons chopped fresh parsley

1 tablespoon chopped fresh basil *or* 1 teaspoon dried basil leaves

½ teaspoon ground cumin

1 clove garlic, finely minced

Salt and freshly ground black pepper

In Dutch oven, heat olive oil over medium-high heat until hot. Add potatoes and onions; cook and stir 5 minutes. Add beef broth, green beans and carrots. Bring mixture to a boil. Cover; reduce heat to low and simmer 10 minutes, stirring occasionally. Add spinach, bell pepper, parsley, basil, cumin and garlic. Cover; simmer an additional 15 to 20 minutes or until potatoes are tender. Season to taste with salt and black pepper. Serve hot.   *Makes 6 to 8 servings*

italian mushroom soup

½ cup dried porcini mushrooms (about ½ ounce)

1 tablespoon olive oil

2 cups chopped onions

8 ounces sliced cremini or button mushrooms

2 cloves garlic, minced

¼ teaspoon dried thyme

¼ cup all-purpose flour

4 cups vegetable broth

½ cup whipping cream

⅓ cup marsala wine (optional)

Salt and black pepper

1. Place dried mushrooms in small bowl; cover with boiling water. Let stand 15 minutes or until tender.

2. Meanwhile, heat oil in large saucepan over medium heat. Add onions; cook 5 minutes or until translucent, stirring occasionally. Add cremini mushrooms, garlic and thyme; cook 8 minutes, stirring occasionally. Add flour; cook and stir 1 minute. Stir in broth.

3. Drain mushrooms, reserving liquid. Chop mushrooms; add to saucepan with reserved liquid. Bring to a boil. Reduce heat to low; simmer 10 minutes. Stir in cream and marsala, if desired. Season with salt and pepper. Simmer 5 minutes or until heated through.

Makes 6 to 8 servings

lentil and brown rice soup

1 envelope LIPTON® RECIPE SECRETS® Onion Soup Mix*

4 cups water

¾ cup lentils, rinsed and drained

½ cup uncooked brown or regular rice

1 can (14½ ounces) whole peeled tomatoes, undrained and coarsely chopped

1 medium carrot, coarsely chopped

1 large stalk celery, coarsely chopped

½ teaspoon dried basil leaves

½ teaspoon dried oregano leaves

¼ teaspoon dried thyme leaves (optional)

1 tablespoon finely chopped fresh parsley

1 tablespoon apple cider vinegar

¼ teaspoon black pepper

Also terrific with LIPTON® RECIPE SECRETS® Beefy Onion Soup Mix.

1. In large saucepan or stockpot, combine soup mix, water, lentils, uncooked rice, tomatoes with liquid, carrot, celery, basil, oregano and thyme.

2. Bring to a boil, then simmer covered, stirring occasionally, 45 minutes or until lentils and rice are tender. Stir in remaining ingredients.

Makes 3 (2-cup) servings

cheesy spinach soup

1 tablespoon soft reduced calorie margarine

¼ cup chopped onions

2 cups fat-free milk

½ pound (8 ounces) VELVEETA® Made With 2% Milk Reduced Fat Pasteurized Prepared Cheese Product, cut into ½-inch cubes

1 package (10 ounces) frozen chopped spinach, cooked, well drained

⅛ teaspoon ground nutmeg

Dash pepper

MELT margarine in medium saucepan on medium heat. Add onions; cook and stir until tender.

ADD remaining ingredients; cook on low heat until VELVEETA® is melted and soup is heated through, stirring occasionally. *Makes 4 servings (about 1 cup each)*

Size-Wise: Savor the flavor of this cheesy soup while keeping portion size in mind.

Substitute: Prepare as directed, substituting frozen chopped broccoli for the spinach.

Use Your Microwave: Microwave onions and margarine in medium microwavable bowl on HIGH 30 seconds to 1 minute or until onions are tender. Stir in remaining ingredients. Microwave 6 to 8 minutes or until VELVEETA® is completely melted and soup is heated through, stirring every 3 minutes.

Prep Time: 15 minutes
Total Time: 25 minutes

 Tip | There are a couple of ways to drain spinach. Squeeze it in between several layers of paper towels. Or place it in a colander over the sink and push the liquid out with the back of a spoon.

cheesy spinach soup

hearty vegetable pasta soup

1 tablespoon vegetable oil

1 small onion, chopped

3 cups vegetable broth

1 can (about 14 ounces) whole tomatoes, undrained, chopped

1 medium unpeeled potato, cubed

2 carrots, sliced

1 stalk celery, sliced

1 teaspoon dried basil

½ teaspoon salt

⅛ teaspoon black pepper

⅓ cup uncooked tiny bow-tie pasta

2 ounces stemmed spinach, chopped

1. Heat oil in Dutch oven or large saucepan over medium-high heat. Add onion; cook and stir until translucent. Add broth, tomatoes with juice, potato, carrots, celery, basil, salt and pepper; bring to a boil over high heat. Reduce heat to low; simmer 20 minutes or until potato and carrots are very tender and flavors are blended, stirring occasionally.

2. Stir in pasta; simmer 8 minutes or until pasta is tender.

3. Stir in spinach; simmer 2 minutes or until spinach is wilted.

Makes 6 servings

cream of asparagus soup

1 tablespoon margarine or butter

1 small onion, chopped

2 cans (14½ ounces each) chicken broth

1 jar (1 pound) RAGÚ® Cheesy!® Classic Alfredo Sauce

2 packages (10 ounces each) frozen asparagus spears, thawed

1. In 3½-quart saucepan, melt margarine over medium heat and cook onion, stirring occasionally, 5 minutes or until tender. Stir in broth, Ragú Cheesy! Sauce and asparagus. Bring to a boil over medium heat, stirring frequently. Reduce heat to low and simmer 5 minutes or until asparagus is tender.

2. In blender or food processor, purée hot soup mixture until smooth. Return soup to saucepan and heat through. Season, if desired, with salt and ground black pepper.

Makes 8 servings

hearty vegetable pasta soup

chile pepper & corn cream chowder

2 tablespoons butter

1 cup chopped onion

2 Anaheim* or poblano chile peppers, seeded and diced

½ cup thinly sliced celery

1 package (16 ounces) frozen corn

12 ounces unpeeled new red potatoes, diced

4 cups whole milk

6 ounces cream cheese, cubed

1 to 2 teaspoons salt

¾ teaspoon black pepper

Anaheim chiles are mild, long narrow green peppers.

1. Melt butter in large saucepan over medium-high heat. Add onion, Anaheim peppers and celery; cook and stir 5 minutes or until onion is translucent.

2. Add corn, potatoes and milk. Bring to a boil. Reduce heat to low; cover and simmer 10 minutes or until potatoes are tender.

3. Remove from heat; add cream cheese, salt and black pepper. Stir until cream cheese is melted.

Makes 4 to 6 servings

chile pepper & corn cream chowder

moroccan lentil & vegetable soup

1 tablespoon olive oil

1 cup chopped onion

4 cloves garlic, minced

½ cup dried lentils, rinsed, sorted and drained

1½ teaspoons ground coriander

1½ teaspoons ground cumin

½ teaspoon ground cinnamon

½ teaspoon black pepper

3¾ cups reduced-sodium vegetable broth

½ cup chopped celery

½ cup chopped sun-dried tomatoes (not packed in oil)

1 yellow squash, chopped

½ cup chopped green bell pepper

1 cup chopped plum tomatoes

½ cup chopped fresh Italian parsley

¼ cup chopped fresh cilantro or basil

1. Heat oil in medium saucepan over medium-high heat. Add onion and garlic; cook and stir 4 minutes or until onion is tender. Stir in lentils, coriander, cumin, cinnamon and black pepper; cook 2 minutes. Add broth, celery and sun-dried tomatoes; bring to a boil. Reduce heat to low; cover and simmer 25 minutes.

2. Stir in squash and bell pepper; cover and cook 10 minutes or until lentils are tender.

3. Top with plum tomatoes, parsley and cilantro just before serving.

Makes 6 servings

 Tip | Many soups taste even better the next day after the flavors have had time to blend. Cover and refrigerate the soup overnight, reserving the plum tomatoes, parsley and cilantro until ready to serve.

moroccan lentil & vegetable soup

spring pea & mint soup

1 tablespoon butter

1 tablespoon vegetable oil

3 small leeks, whites only, cleaned and diced (about 2 cups)

4 cups SWANSON® Chicken Broth (Regular, Natural Goodness® or Certified Organic)

1 medium Yukon Gold potato, diced (about 1 cup)

1 package (16 ounces) frozen peas (3 cups)

½ cup heavy cream or crème fraîche

¼ cup thinly sliced fresh mint leaves

1 cup PEPPERIDGE FARM® Croutons, any variety

1. Heat the butter and oil in a 3-quart saucepan over medium heat. Add the leeks and cook until tender.

2. Stir the broth and potato. Heat to a boil. Reduce the heat to low. Cook for 20 minutes or until the potato is tender.

3. Stir in the peas. Cook for 10 minutes or until the peas are tender.

4. Place ⅓ of the soup mixture into an electric blender or food processor container. Cover and blend until smooth. Pour the mixture into a large bowl. Repeat the blending process twice more with the remaining broth mixture. Return all of the puréed mixture to the saucepan. Add the cream and mint. Cook over medium heat until the mixture is hot. Season to taste.

5. Divide the soup among **6** serving bowls. Top **each** serving of soup with croutons.

Makes 6 servings

Prep Time: 10 minutes
Cook Time: 45 minutes

spring pea & mint soup

two-cheese potato and cauliflower soup

1 tablespoon butter

1 cup chopped onion

2 cloves garlic, minced

5 cups whole milk

1 pound Yukon Gold potatoes, diced

1 pound cauliflower florets

1½ teaspoons salt

⅛ teaspoon ground red pepper

1½ cups (6 ounces) shredded sharp Cheddar cheese

⅓ cup crumbled blue cheese

1. Melt butter in large saucepan over medium-high heat. Add onion; cook and stir 4 minutes or until translucent. Add garlic; cook and stir 15 seconds. Add milk, potatoes, cauliflower, salt and red pepper; bring to a boil. Reduce heat; cover and simmer 15 minutes or until potatoes are tender. Cool slightly.

2. Working in batches, process soup in food processor or blender until smooth. Return to saucepan. Cook and stir over medium heat 2 to 3 minutes or until heated through. Remove from heat; add cheeses. Stir until cheeses are melted.

Makes 4 to 6 servings

 Tip | One pound of trimmed cauliflower will yield about 1½ cups of florets. You can also substitute 1 pound of frozen cauliflower florets for the fresh florets.

two-cheese potato and cauliflower soup

italian skillet roasted vegetable soup

2 tablespoons olive oil, divided

1 medium yellow, red or orange bell pepper, chopped

1 clove garlic, minced

2 cups water

1 can (about 14 ounces) diced tomatoes

1 medium zucchini, thinly sliced

⅛ teaspoon red pepper flakes

1 can (about 15 ounces) navy beans, rinsed and drained

3 to 4 tablespoons chopped fresh basil

1 tablespoon balsamic vinegar

¾ teaspoon salt

½ teaspoon liquid smoke (optional)

Croutons (optional)

1. Heat 1 tablespoon oil in Dutch oven or large saucepan over medium-high heat. Add bell pepper; cook and stir 4 minutes or until edges are browned. Add garlic; cook and stir 15 seconds. Add water, tomatoes, zucchini and red pepper flakes. Bring to a boil over high heat. Reduce heat; cover and simmer 20 minutes.

2. Add beans, basil, remaining 1 tablespoon oil, vinegar, salt and liquid smoke, if desired. Remove from heat. Let stand, covered, 10 minutes before serving. Serve with croutons, if desired.   *Makes 4 servings*

italian skillet roasted vegetable soup

quick
& easy

spicy thai coconut soup

2 cups chicken broth
1 can (14 ounces) light coconut milk
1 tablespoon minced fresh ginger
½ to 1 teaspoon red curry paste
3 cups coarsely shredded cooked chicken (about 12 ounces)
1 can (15 ounces) straw mushrooms, drained
1 can (about 8 ounces) baby corn, drained
2 tablespoons lime juice
¼ cup chopped fresh cilantro

1. Combine broth, coconut milk, ginger and curry in large saucepan. Add chicken, mushrooms and corn. Bring to a simmer over medium heat; cook until heated through.

2. Stir in lime juice. Sprinkle with cilantro before serving.   *Makes 4 servings*

Note: Red curry paste can be found in jars in the Asian food section of large grocery stores. Spice levels can vary between brands. Start with ½ teaspoon, then add more as desired.

spicy thai coconut soup

quick and zesty vegetable soup

1 pound lean ground beef
½ cup chopped onion
Salt and pepper
2 cans (14½ ounces each) DEL MONTE® Italian Recipe Stewed Tomatoes
2 cans (14 ounces each) beef broth
1 can (14½ ounces) DEL MONTE® Mixed Vegetables
½ cup uncooked medium egg noodles
½ teaspoon dried oregano

1. Brown meat with onion in large pot. Cook until onion is tender; drain. Season to taste with salt and pepper.

2. Stir in remaining ingredients. Bring to boil; reduce heat.

3. Cover and simmer 15 minutes or until noodles are tender.   *Makes 8 servings*

new england clam chowder

¼ pound smoked turkey sausage, finely chopped
1½ cups chopped onions
2¾ cups milk
1 medium red potato, diced
1 can (6½ ounces) minced clams, drained, liquid reserved
2 bay leaves
½ teaspoon dried thyme
2 tablespoons butter
¼ teaspoon black pepper
Saltine crackers

1. Spray Dutch oven or large saucepan with nonstick cooking spray; heat over medium-high heat. Add sausage; cook and stir 2 minutes or until browned. Remove from Dutch oven; keep warm.

2. Spray Dutch oven with cooking spray. Add onions; cook and stir 2 minutes. Add milk, potato, reserved clam liquid, bay leaves and thyme. Cover and simmer 15 minutes or until potato is tender.

3. Remove bay leaves. Stir in sausage, clams, butter and pepper. Simmer until heated through, stirring frequently. Crumble crackers over each serving.   *Makes 4 servings*

quick and zesty vegetable soup

hot and sour chicken soup

2 cups water

2 cups chicken broth

1 package (about 10 ounces) refrigerated fully cooked chicken breast strips, cut into pieces

1 package (about 7 ounces) chicken-flavored rice and vermicelli mix

1 jalapeño pepper,* minced

2 green onions, chopped

1 tablespoon soy sauce

1 tablespoon lime juice

1 tablespoon minced fresh cilantro

*Jalapeño peppers can sting and irritate the skin, so wear rubber gloves when handling peppers and do not touch your eyes.

1. Combine water, broth, chicken, rice mix, jalapeño, green onions and soy sauce in large saucepan; bring to a boil over high heat. Reduce heat to low. Cover and simmer 20 minutes or until rice is tender, stirring occasionally.

2. Stir in lime juice and sprinkle with cilantro.   *Makes 4 servings*

velvety vegetable cheese soup

1 package (16 ounces) frozen broccoli, cauliflower and carrot blend

2 cans (14 ounces each) fat-free reduced-sodium chicken broth

¾ pound (12 ounces) VELVEETA® 2% Milk Pasteurized Prepared Cheese Product, cut into ½-inch cubes

BRING combined vegetables and broth to boil in large covered saucepan on medium-high heat. Simmer on low heat 10 minutes or until vegetables are tender.

STIR in VELVEETA®; cook 5 minutes or until VELVEETA® is completely melted and soup is heated through, stirring frequently.   *Makes 6 servings (1 cup each)*

How To Purée Soup: For a smooth consistency, soup can be puréed in a blender or food processor or right in the pan with a hand or immersion blender.

Prep Time: 5 minutes
Total Time: 30 minutes

hot and sour chicken soup

cheeseburger chowder

1 pound ground beef

1 large onion, chopped (about 1 cup)

2 cans (26 ounces each) CAMPBELL'S® Condensed Cream of Mushroom Soup (Regular or 98% Fat Free)

2 soup cans milk

1 cup finely shredded Cheddar cheese (about 4 ounces)

1 cup PEPPERIDGE FARM® Seasoned Croutons

1. Cook the beef and onion in a 3-quart saucepan over medium-high heat until the beef is well browned, stirring often to separate the meat. Pour off any fat.

2. Stir the soup and milk in the saucepan. Cook until the mixture is hot and bubbling. Stir in ½ **cup** cheese. Cook and stir until the cheese is melted.

3. Divide the soup among **8** serving bowls. Top **each** bowl with **1 tablespoon** remaining cheese and **2 tablespoons** croutons. *Makes 8 servings*

roasted corn and chicken soup

4 tablespoons olive oil, divided

1 can (15 ounces) yellow corn, drained

1 can (15 ounces) white corn, drained

1 onion, diced

3 tablespoons ORTEGA® Fire-Roasted Diced Green Chiles

½ of 1½- to 2-pound cooked rotisserie chicken, bones removed and meat shredded

1 packet (1.25 ounces) ORTEGA® 40% Less Sodium Taco Seasoning Mix

4 cups chicken broth

4 ORTEGA® Yellow Corn Taco Shells, crumbled

Heat 2 tablespoons oil over medium heat in large skillet until hot. Add corn. Cook 8 minutes or until browned; stir often to prevent corn from burning. Add remaining 2 tablespoons oil, onion and chiles. Cook and stir 3 minutes longer.

Transfer mixture to large pot. Stir in shredded chicken. Add seasoning mix and toss to combine. Stir in chicken broth and bring to a boil. Reduce heat to low. Simmer 15 minutes. Serve with crumbled taco shells. *Makes 8 servings*

Tip: To make sure the canned corn is well drained, press excess water out with a paper towel.

cheeseburger chowder

zesty chicken & vegetable soup

½ pound boneless skinless chicken breasts, cut into very thin strips

1 to 2 tablespoons *Frank's®️ RedHot®️* Original Cayenne Pepper Sauce

4 cups chicken broth

1 package (16 ounces) frozen stir-fry vegetables

1 cup angel hair pasta or fine egg noodles, broken into 2-inch lengths

1 green onion, thinly sliced

1. Combine chicken and **Frank's RedHot** Sauce in medium bowl; set aside.

2. Heat broth to boiling in large saucepan over medium-high heat. Add vegetables and pasta; return to boiling. Cook 2 minutes. Stir in chicken mixture and green onion. Cook 1 minute or until chicken is no longer pink. *Makes 4 to 6 servings*

Prep Time: 5 minutes
Cook Time: about 8 minutes

Tip | For a change of pace, substitute 6 prepared frozen pot stickers for the pasta. Add to the broth in step 2 and boil until tender.

zesty chicken & vegetable soup

sausage & zucchini soup

1 pound BOB EVANS® Italian Roll Sausage

1 medium onion, diced

1 (28-ounce) can stewed tomatoes

2 (14-ounce) cans beef broth

2 medium zucchini, diced or sliced (about 2 cups)

2 small carrots, diced

2 stalks celery, diced

4 large mushrooms, sliced

   Grated Parmesan cheese for garnish

Crumble and cook sausage and onion in large saucepan over medium heat until sausage is browned. Drain off any drippings. Add remaining ingredients except cheese; simmer, uncovered, over low heat about 40 minutes or until vegetables are tender. Garnish with cheese. Refrigerate leftovers.   *Makes 8 servings*

new orleans fish soup

1 can (about 15 ounces) cannellini beans, rinsed and drained

1 can (about 14 ounces) reduced-sodium chicken broth

1 yellow squash, halved lengthwise and sliced (1 cup)

1 tablespoon Cajun seasoning

1 pound skinless firm fish fillets, such as grouper, cod or haddock, cut into
     1-inch pieces

2 cans (about 14 ounces each) stewed tomatoes

½ cup sliced green onions

1 teaspoon grated orange peel

1. Combine beans, broth, squash and seasoning in large saucepan. Bring to a boil over high heat. Reduce heat to low.

2. Stir in fish and tomatoes; cover and simmer 3 to 5 minutes or until fish just begins to flake when tested with fork. Stir in green onions and orange peel just before serving.
          Makes 4 servings

sausage & zucchini soup

creamy tuscan bean & chicken soup

2 cans (10¾ ounces each) CAMPBELL'S® Condensed Cream of Celery Soup (Regular or 98% Fat Free)

2 cups water

1 can (about 15 ounces) white kidney beans (cannellini), rinsed and drained

1 can (about 14½ ounces) diced tomatoes, undrained

2 cups shredded or diced cooked chicken

¼ cup bacon bits

3 ounces fresh baby spinach leaves (about 3 cups)

Olive oil

Grated or shredded Parmesan cheese

1. Heat the soup, water, beans, tomatoes, chicken and bacon in a 3-quart saucepan over medium-high heat to a boil.

2. Stir in the spinach. Cook for 5 minutes or until the spinach is wilted. Serve the soup with a drizzle of oil and sprinkle with the cheese.   *Makes 4 to 6 servings*

Kitchen Tip: For the shredded chicken, purchase a rotisserie chicken. Remove the skin and bones. You can either shred the chicken with your fingers or use 2 forks.

Prep Time: 10 minutes
Cook Time: 10 minutes

creamy tuscan bean & chicken soup

super simple tortilla soup

2 cans (14 ounces) chicken broth

1 can (14.5 ounces) HUNT'S® Diced Tomatoes, undrained

1 cup frozen whole kernel corn

1½ cups shredded cooked chicken

1 teaspoon chipotle-flavored hot pepper sauce

1 cup tortilla chips, broken

Shredded Cheddar cheese, sliced green onions, cilantro sprigs and chopped peeled avocado, if desired

1. Combine broth, tomatoes with their juice and corn in medium saucepan.

2. Bring to a boil over high heat. Reduce heat to low. Add chicken and hot pepper sauce; mix well. Simmer 5 minutes or until heated through, stirring occasionally.

3. Top with tortilla chips. Garnish with cheese, onions, cilantro and avocados, if desired. *Makes 6 servings (1 cup each)*

Prep Time: 15 minutes
Cook Time: 15 minutes

creamy artichoke soup

1 jar (about 6 ounces) marinated artichoke hearts, undrained

1 cup chopped onion

2 cloves garlic, minced

2 tablespoons all-purpose flour

2 cans (10½ ounces each) condensed chicken broth, undiluted, divided

1 cup milk

1. Drain marinade from artichoke hearts into large saucepan; set artichoke hearts aside. Add onion and garlic to saucepan; cover and cook over low heat 10 minutes or until onion is tender. Blend in flour. Slowly stir in 1 can broth. Bring to a boil over medium heat; cook 1 minute or until mixture thickens, stirring constantly.

2. Process artichoke hearts in food processor or blender until smooth. Strain into saucepan. Add remaining 1 can broth and milk. Cook and stir over low heat until heated through. *Do not boil.* *Makes 4 servings*

spicy curried squash soup

½ **cup chopped onion**

 1 **tablespoon butter or olive oil**

¾ **teaspoon curry powder**

 2 **packages (12 ounces each) frozen butternut squash, thawed**

 4 **cups vegetable broth**

 1 **cup frozen sliced carrots, thawed**

 3 **to 4 tablespoons** *Frank's® RedHot®* **Original Cayenne Pepper Sauce**

1. Sauté onion in butter in large saucepan until tender. Stir in curry powder and cook 1 minute. Add remaining ingredients; simmer 10 minutes or until carrots are tender.

2. Place 2 cups of the soup into blender container. Cover and process on low speed until smooth.* Transfer to bowl. Repeat with remaining soup mixture. Return all to saucepan.

3. Heat through. If desired, serve with a dollop of sour cream.

Makes 6 servings (about 6 cups)

Caution! Soup mixture will be hot. Place kitchen towel over blender before blending. A hand-held immersion blender may be used instead of the blender.

Prep Time: 5 minutes
Cook Time: 10 minutes

 Tip | Curry powder is actually a mixture of several spices. Different brands may include different seasonings and some cooks even prepare their own blends. Spices may include coriander, cumin, black, red or white pepper, fenugreek, fennel, nutmeg, ginger, cardamom, cloves, cinnamon, bay leaf, saffron, lemongrass, and/or turmeric.

sensational chicken noodle soup

4 cups SWANSON® Chicken Broth (Regular, Natural Goodness® or Certified Organic)
Generous dash ground black pepper
1 medium carrot, sliced (about ½ cup)
1 stalk celery, sliced (about ½ cup)
½ cup uncooked medium egg noodles
1 cup cubed cooked chicken or turkey

1. Heat the broth, black pepper, carrot and celery in a 2-quart saucepan over medium-high heat to a boil.

2. Stir in the noodles and chicken. Reduce the heat to medium. Cook for 10 minutes or until the noodles are tender but still firm. *Makes 4 servings*

Prep Time: 5 minutes
Cook Time: 20 minutes

quick & easy meatball soup

1 package (15 to 18 ounces) frozen Italian sausage meatballs without sauce
2 cans (about 14 ounces each) Italian-style stewed tomatoes
2 cans (about 14 ounces each) beef broth
1 can (about 14 ounces) mixed vegetables
½ cup uncooked rotini pasta or small macaroni
½ teaspoon dried oregano

1. Thaw meatballs in microwave according to package directions.

2. Combine meatballs, tomatoes, broth, vegetables, pasta and oregano in large saucepan. Bring to a boil. Reduce heat; cover and simmer 15 minutes or until pasta is tender. *Makes 4 to 6 servings*

sensational chicken noodle soup

a-b-c minestrone

1 tablespoon olive oil

1 medium onion, chopped

2 medium carrots, chopped

1 small zucchini, chopped

½ teaspoon dried Italian seasoning

4 cups chicken broth

1 jar (1 pound 10 ounces) RAGÚ® Old World Style® Pasta Sauce

1 can (15½ ounces) cannellini or white kidney beans, rinsed and drained

1 cup alphabet pasta

1. In 4-quart saucepan, heat olive oil over medium heat and cook onion, carrots and zucchini, stirring frequently, 5 minutes or until vegetables are tender. Add Italian seasoning and cook, stirring occasionally, 1 minute. Add broth and Pasta Sauce and bring to a boil. Stir in beans and pasta. Cook, stirring occasionally, 10 minutes or until pasta is tender.

2. Serve, if desired, with chopped parsley and grated Parmesan cheese.

Makes 8 servings

chicken corn chowder with cheese

2 tablespoons butter or margarine

⅓ cup chopped celery

⅓ cup chopped red bell pepper

1½ tablespoons all-purpose flour

2 cups milk

1 can (14¾ ounces) cream-style corn

1⅓ cups *French's*® French Fried Onions, divided

1 cup diced cooked chicken

2 tablespoons chopped green chilies

½ cup (2 ounces) shredded Cheddar cheese

1. Melt butter in 3-quart saucepan over medium-high heat. Sauté celery and bell pepper 3 minutes or until crisp-tender. Blend in flour; cook 1 minute, stirring constantly. Gradually stir in milk and corn. Bring to a boil. Reduce heat; simmer 4 minutes or until thickened, stirring frequently.

2. Add **⅔ cup** French Fried Onions, chicken and chilies. Cook until heated through. Spoon soup into serving bowls; sprinkle with remaining onions and cheese. Splash on **Frank's RedHot** Sauce to taste, if desired.

Makes 4 servings

a-b-c minestrone

chicken tortellini soup

6 cups chicken broth

1 package (9 ounces) refrigerated cheese and spinach tortellini

1 package (about 6 ounces) refrigerated fully cooked chicken breast strips, cut into bite-size pieces

2 cups baby spinach

4 to 6 tablespoons grated Parmesan cheese

1 tablespoon chopped fresh chives *or* 2 tablespoons sliced green onion

1. Bring broth to a boil in large saucepan over high heat; add tortellini. Reduce heat to medium; cook 5 minutes. Stir in chicken and spinach.

2. Reduce heat to low; cook 3 minutes or until chicken is heated through. Sprinkle with Parmesan cheese and chives.

Makes 4 servings

swanson® chicken vegetable soup

3 cans (14 ounces each) SWANSON® Natural Goodness® Chicken Broth (5¼ cups)

½ teaspoon dried thyme leaves, crushed

¼ teaspoon garlic powder or 2 cloves garlic, minced

2 cups frozen whole kernel corn

1 package (about 10 ounces) frozen cut green beans

1 cup cut-up canned tomatoes

1 stalk celery, chopped

2 cups cubed cooked chicken or turkey

1. Mix broth, thyme, garlic, corn, beans, tomatoes and celery in saucepot. Heat to a boil. Cover and cook over low heat 5 minutes or until vegetables are tender.

2. Add chicken and heat through.

Makes 6 servings

Prep Time: 10 minutes
Cook Time: 15 minutes

chicken tortellini soup

cheesy mexican soup

1 cup chopped onion

1 tablespoon vegetable oil

2 cups milk

1 can (about 14 ounces) chicken broth

1 container (13 ounces) ORTEGA® Salsa & Cheese Bowl

1 can (7 ounces) ORTEGA® Fire-Roasted Diced Green Chiles

4 ORTEGA® Taco Shells, crushed

¼ cup chopped cilantro

Cook and stir onion in oil in large saucepan over medium-high heat for 4 to 6 minutes until tender. Reduce heat to medium-low.

Stir in milk, chicken broth, Salsa & Cheese and green chiles; cook for 5 to 7 minutes until hot, stirring frequently.

Microwave crushed taco shells on HIGH (100%) 30 to 45 seconds. Cool. Serve soup sprinkled with crushed taco shells and cilantro. *Makes 8 servings*

asian chicken noodle bowl

4 *Tyson®* Fresh Boneless Skinless Chicken Thighs

¾ teaspoon Chinese five-spice powder

¼ teaspoon black pepper

⅛ teaspoon salt

2 teaspoons vegetable oil

2 cloves garlic, finely chopped

3 cans (14 ounces each) reduced-sodium chicken broth

1 tablespoon soy sauce

1 package (9 ounces) fresh angel hair pasta

1 bag (6 ounces) baby spinach

1. Combine five-spice powder, pepper and salt in cup. Wash hands. Cut chicken into 1-inch pieces. Rub spices onto chicken. Wash hands.

2. Heat oil in 2-quart saucepan over medium-high heat. Add chicken and cook about 5 minutes or until browned on all sides. Add garlic and cook about 1 minute or until fragrant. Add chicken broth and soy sauce; cover and bring to a boil. Uncover, reduce heat to simmer and cook 3 minutes. Add pasta; simmer 1 minute or until tender. Add spinach; stir just until wilted. Refrigerate leftovers immediately.

Makes 4 servings

cheesy mexican soup

ravioli soup

1 package (9 ounces) fresh or frozen cheese ravioli or tortellini
¾ pound hot Italian sausage, crumbled
1 can (14½ ounces) DEL MONTE® Italian Recipe Stewed Tomatoes
1 can (14½ ounces) beef broth
1 can (14½ ounces) DEL MONTE® Cut Italian Green Beans, drained
2 green onions, sliced

1. Cook pasta according to package directions; drain.

2. Meanwhile, cook sausage in 5-quart pot over medium-high heat until no longer pink; drain. Add undrained tomatoes, broth and 1¾ cups water; bring to a boil.

3. Reduce heat to low; stir in pasta, beans and green onions. Simmer until heated through. Season with pepper and sprinkle with grated Parmesan cheese, if desired.

Makes 4 servings

Prep and Cook Time: 15 minutes

egg drop soup

2 cans (about 14 ounces each) reduced-sodium chicken or vegetable broth
1 tablespoon reduced-sodium soy sauce
2 teaspoons cornstarch
2 eggs, beaten
¼ cup thinly sliced green onions

1. Bring broth to a boil in large saucepan over high heat. Reduce heat to a simmer.

2. Stir soy sauce into cornstarch in small bowl until smooth; stir into broth. Cook and stir 2 minutes or until soup thickens slightly.

3. Stirring constantly in one direction, slowly pour eggs in thin stream into soup. Sprinkle each serving with green onions. *Makes 2 to 4 servings*

ravioli soup

pasta fagioli

1 jar (1 pound 10 ounces) RAGÚ® Chunky Gardenstyle Pasta Sauce
1 can (19 ounces) white kidney beans, rinsed and drained
1 box (10 ounces) frozen chopped spinach, thawed
8 ounces ditalini pasta, cooked and drained (reserve 2 cups pasta water)

1. In 6-quart saucepot, combine Pasta Sauce, beans, spinach, pasta and reserved pasta water; heat through.

2. Season, if desired, with salt, ground black pepper and grated Parmesan cheese.

Makes 4 servings

Prep Time: 20 minutes
Cook Time: 10 minutes

1–2–3 steak soup

1 pound boneless beef sirloin steak, cut into 1-inch cubes
1 tablespoon vegetable oil
½ pound sliced mushrooms (about 2½ cups)
2 cups *French's*® French Fried Onions, divided
1 package (16 ounces) frozen vegetables for stew (potatoes, carrots, celery and pearl onions)
2 cans (14½ ounces each) beef broth
1 can (8 ounces) tomato sauce
1 tablespoon *French's*® Worcestershire Sauce
Garnish: chopped parsley (optional)

1. Cook beef in hot oil in large saucepan over medium heat until browned, stirring frequently. Remove beef from pan; set aside.

2. Sauté mushrooms and **½ cup** French Fried Onions in drippings in same pan over medium heat until golden, stirring occasionally. Stir in vegetables, broth, tomato sauce and Worcestershire. Return beef to pan.

3. Heat to a boil over high heat; reduce heat to low. Cover and simmer 20 minutes or until vegetables are tender, stirring occasionally. Spoon soup into serving bowls; top with remaining onions. Garnish with chopped parsley, if desired.   *Makes 8 servings*

Prep Time: 5 minutes
Cook Time: 30 minutes

pasta fagioli

sweet potato bisque with ginger

 2 cans (15 ounces each) sweet potatoes in heavy syrup, drained
 1 can (14 ounces) coconut milk
 1 cup vegetable or chicken broth
 1 green onion, cut into thirds
 ¼ teaspoon salt
 ⅛ teaspoon ground red pepper
 2 teaspoons grated fresh ginger or crystallized ginger, plus additional for garnish
   Chives (optional)

1. Combine sweet potatoes, coconut milk, broth, green onion, salt and ground red pepper in food processor or blender; process until smooth.

2. Transfer to large saucepan. Bring to a boil, stirring frequently. Reduce heat to low; simmer 3 minutes. Remove from heat; stir in ginger. Garnish with additional ginger and chives. *Makes 4 servings*

main-dish chicken soup

 6 cups reduced-sodium chicken broth
 1 cup grated carrots
 ½ cup diced red bell pepper
 ½ cup frozen green peas
 ½ cup sliced green onions
 1 seedless cucumber
 12 chicken tenders (about 1 pound), halved
 ½ teaspoon white pepper

1. Bring broth to a boil in Dutch oven or large saucepan. Add carrots, bell pepper, peas and green onions. Return to a boil. Reduce heat; simmer 3 minutes.

2. Meanwhile, cut ends off cucumber and discard. Using vegetable peeler, start at top and make long, noodle-like strips of cucumber. Cut any remaining cucumber pieces into thin slices. Add cucumber to Dutch oven; cook 2 minutes over low heat.

3. Add chicken and white pepper; simmer 5 minutes or until chicken is cooked through. *Makes 6 servings*

sweet potato bisque with ginger

global
flavors

black & white mexican bean soup

1 tablespoon vegetable oil

1 cup chopped onion

½ teaspoon POLANER® Minced Garlic

¼ cup all-purpose flour

1 packet (1.25 ounces) ORTEGA® Taco Seasoning Mix

2 cups milk

1 can (about 14 ounces) chicken broth

1 package (16 ounces) frozen corn

1 can (15 ounces) JOAN OF ARC® Great Northern Beans, rinsed, drained

1 can (15 ounces) ORTEGA® Black Beans, rinsed, drained

1 can (4 ounces) ORTEGA® Fire-Roasted Diced Green Chiles

2 tablespoons chopped cilantro

Heat oil in large pan or Dutch oven over medium-high heat. Add onion and garlic; cook until onion is tender.

Stir in flour and taco seasoning mix; gradually stir in milk until blended. Add remaining ingredients except cilantro.

Bring to a boil, stirring constantly. Reduce heat to low; simmer for 15 minutes or until thickened, stirring occasionally.

Stir in cilantro.   *Makes 6 servings*

black & white mexican bean soup

west african vegetable soup

2 tablespoons olive oil

1 large sweet onion, sliced (about 2 cups)

2 cloves garlic, minced

4 cups SWANSON® Vegetable or Chicken Broth (Regular or Certified Organic)

½ teaspoon ground cinnamon

½ teaspoon crushed red pepper

2 medium sweet potatoes, peeled, cut in half lengthwise and sliced (2 cups)

1 can (14½ ounces) diced tomatoes, undrained

½ cup raisins

1 bag (6 ounces) spinach, stemmed and coarsely chopped (about 4 cups)

1 can (about 16 ounces) chickpeas (garbanzo beans), rinsed and drained

Cooked couscous (optional)

1. Heat the oil in a 6-quart saucepot over medium heat. Add the onion and garlic and cook until tender.

2. Add the broth, cinnamon, red pepper, sweet potatoes, tomatoes and raisins. Heat to a boil. Reduce the heat to low. Cover and cook for 20 minutes or until the potatoes are tender.

3. Add the spinach and chickpeas. Cook until the spinach wilts.

4. Divide soup among **6** serving bowls. Place about ½ **cup** of the couscous on top of **each** bowl of soup, if desired.   *Makes 6 servings*

Prep Time: 15 minutes
Cook Time: 30 minutes

west african vegetable soup

tofu and snow pea noodle bowl

5 cups water

6 tablespoons chicken-flavored broth powder*

4 ounces uncooked vermicelli, broken in thirds

½ pound firm tofu, patted dry and cut in ¼-inch cubes

1 cup (3 ounces) fresh snow peas

1 cup matchstick-size carrot strips

½ teaspoon chili garlic sauce

½ cup chopped green onions

¼ cup chopped fresh cilantro (optional)

2 tablespoons lime juice

1 tablespoon grated fresh ginger

2 teaspoons soy sauce

*Chicken-flavored vegetarian broth powder can be found in natural food stores and some supermarkets.

1. Bring water to a boil in large saucepan over high heat. Stir in broth powder and vermicelli. Return to a boil. Reduce heat to medium; simmer 6 minutes. Stir in tofu, snow peas, carrots and chili garlic sauce; simmer 2 minutes.

2. Remove from heat; stir in green onions, cilantro, if desired, lime juice, ginger and soy sauce. Serve immediately.   *Makes 4 servings*

 Tip | Substitute 5 cups of canned vegetable broth for the water and broth powder.

tofu and snow pea noodle bowl

japanese noodle soup

1 package (about 8 ounces) Japanese udon noodles

1 teaspoon vegetable oil

1 medium red bell pepper, cut into thin strips

1 medium carrot, diagonally sliced

2 green onions, thinly sliced

2 cans (about 14 ounces each) reduced-sodium vegetable or beef broth

1 cup water

1 teaspoon soy sauce

½ teaspoon grated fresh ginger

½ teaspoon black pepper

2 cups thinly sliced fresh shiitake mushrooms, stems removed

4 ounces daikon (Japanese radish), peeled and cut into thin strips

4 ounces firm tofu, drained and cut into ½-inch cubes

1. Cook noodles according to package directions. Drain; set aside and keep warm.

2. Meanwhile, heat oil in wok or large saucepan over medium-high heat. Add bell pepper, carrot and green onions; cook 3 minutes or until slightly softened. Stir in broth, water, soy sauce, ginger and black pepper; bring to a boil. Add mushrooms, daikon and tofu; reduce heat and simmer 5 minutes.

3. Place noodles in bowls; ladle soup over noodles.   *Makes 6 servings*

indonesian curried soup

1 can (14 ounces) coconut milk*

1 can (10¾ ounces) condensed tomato soup

¾ cup milk

3 tablespoons *Frank's® RedHot®* Original Cayenne Pepper Sauce

1½ teaspoons curry powder

You can substitute 1 cup half-and-half for coconut milk BUT increase milk to 1½ cups.

1. Combine all ingredients in medium saucepan; stir until smooth.

2. Cook over low heat about 5 minutes or until heated through, stirring occasionally.

Makes 6 servings (4 cups)

Prep Time: 5 minutes
Cook Time: 5 minutes

japanese noodle soup

middle eastern lentil soup

1 cup dried lentils
2 tablespoons olive oil
1 small onion, chopped
1 medium red bell pepper, chopped
1 teaspoon whole fennel seeds
½ teaspoon ground cumin
¼ teaspoon ground red pepper
4 cups water
½ teaspoon salt
1 tablespoon lemon juice
½ cup plain yogurt
2 tablespoons chopped fresh parsley

1. Rinse lentils, discarding any debris or blemished lentils; drain and set aside.

2. Heat oil in large saucepan over medium-high heat. Add onion and bell pepper; cook and stir 5 minutes or until tender. Add fennel seeds, cumin and ground red pepper; cook and stir 1 minute.

3. Add water, lentils and salt. Bring to a boil. Reduce heat to low. Cover and simmer 25 to 30 minutes or until lentils are tender. Stir in lemon juice.

4. Top each serving with yogurt; sprinkle with parsley.   *Makes 4 servings*

 Tip | Serve with homemade pita chips. Cut 4 pita bread rounds into 6 wedges each. Toss wedges with 1 tablespoon olive oil and 1 teaspoon coarse salt; spread on large baking sheet. Bake at 350°F 15 minutes or until light brown and crisp.

middle eastern lentil soup

beef soup with noodles

2 tablespoons soy sauce

1 teaspoon minced fresh ginger

¼ teaspoon red pepper flakes

1 boneless beef top sirloin steak (about ¾ pound)

1 tablespoon peanut or vegetable oil

2 cups sliced fresh mushrooms

2 cans (about 14 ounces each) beef broth

1 cup (3 ounces) fresh snow peas, cut diagonally into 1-inch pieces

1½ cups hot cooked egg noodles (2 ounces uncooked)

1 green onion, cut diagonally into thin slices

1 teaspoon dark sesame oil (optional)

Red bell pepper strips (optional)

1. Combine soy sauce, ginger and red pepper flakes in small bowl. Spread mixture evenly over both sides of steak. Marinate 15 minutes.

2. Heat peanut oil in deep skillet over medium-high heat. Drain steak; reserve marinade (there will only be a small amount of marinade). Add steak to skillet; cook 5 minutes per side for medium-rare or until desired doneness. Let stand on cutting board 10 minutes.

3. Add mushrooms to skillet; cook and stir 2 minutes. Add broth, snow peas and reserved marinade; bring to a boil, scraping up browned bits. Reduce heat to low; stir in noodles.

4. Cut steak lengthwise in half, then crosswise into thin slices. Stir into soup; heat through. Stir in green onion and sesame oil, if desired. Garnish with bell pepper strips.

Makes 4 to 6 servings

beef soup with noodles

greek lemon and rice soup

 2 tablespoons butter
⅓ cup minced green onions
 6 cups vegetable or chicken broth
⅔ cup uncooked long grain white rice
 4 eggs
   Juice of 1 lemon
⅛ teaspoon white pepper
   Lemon peel strips (optional)

1. Melt butter in large saucepan over medium heat. Add green onions; cook and stir 3 minutes or until tender.

2. Stir in broth and rice. Bring to a boil over high heat. Reduce heat to low; cover and simmer 20 to 25 minutes or until rice is tender.

3. Whisk eggs in medium bowl. Whisk in lemon juice and ½ cup broth mixture. Stirring constantly in one direction, slowly pour egg mixture in thin stream into soup. Cook and stir over low heat 2 to 3 minutes or until soup thickens enough to lightly coat spoon. *Do not boil.*

4. Stir in pepper. Garnish with lemon peel. *Makes 6 to 8 servings*

shantung twin mushroom soup

 1 package (1 ounce) dried shiitake mushrooms
 2 teaspoons vegetable oil
 1 large onion, coarsely chopped
 2 cloves garlic, minced
 2 cups sliced button mushrooms
 2 cans (about 14 ounces each) reduced-sodium chicken broth
 2 ounces cooked ham, cut into thin slivers
½ cup thinly sliced green onions
 1 tablespoon dry sherry
 1 tablespoon reduced-sodium soy sauce
 1 tablespoon cornstarch

1. Place dried mushrooms in small bowl; cover with boiling water. Soak 20 minutes to soften. Drain; squeeze out excess water. Discard stems; slice caps.

continued on page 194

greek lemon and rice soup

2. Heat oil in large saucepan over medium heat. Add chopped onion and garlic; cook 1 minute. Add dried and button mushrooms; cook and stir 4 minutes.

3. Add broth; bring to a boil over high heat. Reduce heat to medium; cover and simmer 15 minutes.

4. Stir in ham and green onions; cook until heated through. Stir sherry and soy sauce into cornstarch in small bowl until smooth; stir into soup. Cook 2 minutes or until soup is thickened, stirring occasionally. *Makes 6 servings*

hearty caribbean-style soup

1 tablespoon vegetable oil

2 boneless pork chops (about ½ pound), cut into ½-inch pieces

½ pound smoked sausage, cut lengthwise in half and sliced ¼ inch thick (about 1½ cups)

1 medium onion, chopped (about 1 cup)

2 cloves garlic, minced

7 cups SWANSON® Chicken Broth (Regular, Natural Goodness® or Certified Organic)

1 teaspoon Caribbean jerk seasoning

2 medium sweet potatoes, peeled and cut into 1-inch pieces (about 2 cups)

2 cups loosely packed baby spinach leaves or 2 cups coarsely chopped beet tops

1. Heat the oil in a 4-quart saucepan over medium-high heat. Cook the pork, sausage, onion and garlic for 5 minutes or until the onion is tender-crisp.

2. Stir in the broth, seasoning and sweet potatoes. Heat to a boil. Reduce the heat to low. Cover and cook for 10 minutes.

3. Stir in the spinach. Cook for 5 minutes more or until the potatoes are tender.
Makes 6 servings

Prep Time: 20 minutes
Cook Time: 25 minutes

hearty caribbean-style soup

vietnamese beef soup

¾ pound boneless beef top sirloin or top round steak

3 cups water

1 can (about 14 ounces) beef broth

1 can (10½ ounces) condensed beef consommé, undiluted

2 tablespoons reduced-sodium soy sauce

2 tablespoons minced fresh ginger

1 cinnamon stick (3 inches long)

4 ounces rice noodles (rice sticks), about ⅛ inch wide

½ cup matchstick-size carrot strips

2 cups fresh bean sprouts

1 small red onion, halved and thinly sliced

½ cup chopped fresh cilantro

½ cup chopped fresh basil

2 jalapeño peppers,* minced *or* 1 to 3 teaspoons Chinese chili sauce or paste

Jalapeño peppers can sting and irritate the skin, so wear rubber gloves when handling peppers and do not touch your eyes.

1. Freeze beef 45 minutes or until firm.

2. Combine water, broth, consommé, soy sauce, ginger and cinnamon stick in large saucepan; bring to a boil over high heat. Reduce heat to low; cover and simmer 20 minutes. Remove cinnamon stick; discard. Meanwhile, place noodles in large bowl and cover with warm water; let stand 20 minutes or until softened.

3. Drain noodles; add to broth with carrots. Cook 2 to 3 minutes or until noodles are tender. Slice beef lengthwise in half, then crosswise into very thin strips. Add beef and bean sprouts to soup; cook 1 minute or until beef is no longer pink.

4. Remove from heat; stir in red onion, cilantro, basil and jalapeño peppers.

Makes 6 servings

indian carrot soup

⅔ **cup chopped onion (about 1 small)**

1 **tablespoon minced fresh ginger**

1 **teaspoon olive oil**

1½ **teaspoons curry powder**

½ **teaspoon ground cumin**

2 **cans (about 14 ounces each) reduced-sodium vegetable or chicken broth, divided**

1 **pound baby carrots**

1 **tablespoon sugar**

¼ **teaspoon ground cinnamon**

Pinch ground red pepper

2 **teaspoons fresh lime juice**

3 **tablespoons chopped fresh cilantro**

¼ **cup plain yogurt**

1. Spray large saucepan with nonstick cooking spray; heat over medium heat. Add onion and ginger; reduce heat to low. Cover and cook 3 to 4 minutes or until onion is transparent and crisp-tender, stirring occasionally.

2. Add oil; cook and stir 3 to 4 minutes or until onion is golden. Add curry powder and cumin; cook and stir 30 seconds or until fragrant. Add 1 can broth and carrots; bring to a boil over high heat. Reduce heat to low; cover and simmer 15 minutes or until carrots are tender.

3. Blend carrot mixture in blender or food processor until smooth; return to saucepan. Stir in remaining 1 can broth, sugar, cinnamon and red pepper; bring to a boil over medium heat. Remove from heat; stir in lime juice. Sprinkle each serving with cilantro and yogurt.

Makes 4 servings

brazilian black bean soup

1 red onion, chopped

2 cloves garlic, minced

1 can (29 ounces) black beans, drained

1 can (14½ ounces) vegetable or chicken broth

3 tablespoons *Frank's® RedHot®* Original Cayenne Pepper Sauce

2 tablespoons chopped cilantro

2 teaspoons ground cumin

2 tablespoons rum or sherry (optional)

1. Heat **1 tablespoon oil** in 3-quart saucepot. Cook and stir onion and garlic 3 minutes or just until tender. Stir in **1½ cups water** and remaining ingredients *except* rum. Heat to boiling. Reduce heat to medium-low. Cook, partially covered, 20 minutes or until flavors are blended, stirring occasionally.

2. Ladle about half of soup into blender or food processor. Cover securely. Blend on low speed until mixture is smooth. Return to saucepot. Stir in rum. Cook over medium-low heat 3 minutes or until heated through and flavors are blended. Garnish with lime slices, sour cream, minced onion or cilantro, if desired.   *Makes 4 to 6 servings*

Prep Time: 10 minutes
Cook Time: 30 minutes

 Tip | Cilantro is also known as coriander or Chinese parsley. It is sold in bunches in the produce section of the grocery store. Cilantro should be stored in the refrigerator in a plastic bag or in a glass of water. It usually stays fresh for about 1 week.

wonton soup

¼ pound ground pork, chicken or turkey

¼ cup finely chopped water chestnuts

2 tablespoons soy sauce, divided

1 egg white, lightly beaten

1 teaspoon minced fresh ginger

12 wonton wrappers

6 cups chicken broth

1½ cups stemmed spinach, torn

1 cup thinly sliced cooked pork (optional)

½ cup diagonally sliced green onions

1 tablespoon dark sesame oil

Shredded carrot (optional)

1. For wonton filling, combine ground pork, water chestnuts, 1 tablespoon soy sauce, egg white and ginger in small bowl; mix well.

2. Place 1 wonton wrapper with point toward edge of counter. Mound 1 teaspoon filling near bottom point. Fold bottom point over filling, then roll wrapper over once. Moisten inside points with water. Bring side points together below filling, overlapping slightly; press together firmly to seal. Repeat with remaining wrappers and filling.* Keep finished wontons covered with plastic wrap while filling remaining wrappers.

3. Combine broth and remaining 1 tablespoon soy sauce in large saucepan. Bring to a boil over high heat. Reduce heat to medium; add wontons. Simmer 4 minutes or until filling is cooked through.

4. Stir in spinach, sliced pork, if desired, and green onions; remove from heat. Stir in sesame oil. Garnish each serving with shredded carrot. *Makes 4 servings*

*Wontons may be made ahead to this point; cover and refrigerate up to 8 hours or freeze up to 3 months. Proceed as directed above if using refrigerated wontons; increase simmering time to 6 minutes if using frozen wontons.

wonton soup

spanish chicken and rice soup

2 tablespoons vegetable oil

1 pound skinless, boneless chicken thighs, cut into cubes

1 large sweet onion, chopped (about 2 cups)

2 cloves garlic, minced

¼ teaspoon crushed red pepper

8 cups SWANSON® Chicken Broth (Regular, Natural Goodness® or Certified Organic)

1 can (14½ ounces) diced tomatoes, undrained

1 package (5 ounces) saffron yellow rice mix with seasoning

½ cup pitted green olives, sliced

¼ cup shredded fresh basil leaves

1. Heat **1 tablespoon** of the oil in a 6-quart saucepot over medium-high heat. Add the chicken and cook until it's well browned, stirring often. Remove the chicken from the saucepot with a slotted spoon.

2. Add the remaining oil to the saucepot and reduce the heat to medium. Add the onion, garlic and red pepper and cook for 3 minutes.

3. Stir in the broth and tomatoes. Heat to a boil. Reduce the heat to low. Cover and cook for 15 minutes.

4. Stir in the rice and olives. Return the chicken to the saucepot. Cover and cook for 20 minutes or until the chicken is cooked through and the rice is done. Stir in the basil. Garnish with additional basil, if desired.   *Makes 6 servings*

Kitchen Tip: To shred fresh basil, select leaves that are not bruised or wilted. Stack the leaves and roll up. Slice with a sharp knife into very thin slices.

Prep Time: 15 minutes
Cook Time: 50 minutes

spanish chicken and rice soup

short rib soup (kalbitang)

2 pounds beef short ribs
2 quarts (8 cups) water
2 tablespoons dried cloud ear or other Oriental mushrooms
½ cup thinly sliced green onions
3 tablespoons soy sauce
2 tablespoons Sesame Salt (recipe follows)
1 tablespoon slivered garlic (about 2 cloves)
½ teaspoon dark sesame oil
¼ teaspoon red pepper flakes
1 egg, lightly beaten
1 bunch chives

1. Score both sides of short ribs in diamond pattern with tip of sharp knife.

2. Bring ribs and water to a boil in Dutch oven or large saucepan over high heat. Reduce heat to low; cook, uncovered, about 1½ hours or until meat is tender. Remove ribs from broth. Skim fat from broth.

3. Meanwhile, place mushrooms in small bowl; cover with hot water. Let stand 30 minutes or until caps are soft. Drain; squeeze out excess water. Discard stems; slice caps.

4. Cut meat into bite-size pieces. Add beef, mushrooms, green onions, soy sauce, Sesame Salt, garlic, sesame oil and red pepper flakes to broth; cook 15 minutes over low heat.

5. Meanwhile, spray small omelet pan or skillet with nonstick cooking spray. Pour egg into pan; cook over medium-high heat until set on both sides. Cut omelet into strips. Garnish each serving with omelet strips and chives.   *Makes 4 servings*

Sesame Salt: Heat small skillet over medium heat. Add ½ cup sesame seeds; cook and stir about 3 minutes or until seeds are golden. Cool. Crush toasted sesame seeds and ¼ teaspoon salt with mortar and pestle or process in clean coffee or spice grinder. Store leftovers in refrigerator in covered glass jar.

short rib soup (kalbitang)

hot and sour soup

1 package (1 ounce) dried shiitake mushrooms

4 cups chicken broth

3 tablespoons white vinegar

2 tablespoons soy sauce

½ to 1 teaspoon hot chili oil

¼ teaspoon white pepper

¼ pound firm tofu, patted dry and cut into ½-inch cubes

1 cup shredded cooked pork, chicken or turkey

½ cup drained canned bamboo shoots, cut into thin strips

3 tablespoons water

2 tablespoons cornstarch

1 egg white, lightly beaten

¼ cup thinly sliced green onions or chopped fresh cilantro

1 teaspoon dark sesame oil

1. Place mushrooms in small bowl; cover with warm water. Let stand 20 minutes to soften. Drain; squeeze out excess water. Discard stems; slice caps.

2. Meanwhile, combine broth, vinegar, soy sauce, chili oil and white pepper in medium saucepan. Bring to a boil over high heat. Reduce heat to low; simmer 2 minutes.

3. Stir in mushrooms, tofu, pork and bamboo shoots; cook and stir until heated through.

4. Stir water into cornstarch in small bowl until smooth. Stir into soup until blended. Cook and stir 4 minutes or until soup boils and thickens. Remove from heat.

5. Stirring constantly in one direction, slowly pour egg white in thin stream into soup. Stir in green onions and sesame oil.   *Makes 4 to 6 servings*

hot and sour soup

albondigas soup

1 pound ground beef

2 eggs, lightly beaten

¼ cup blue or yellow cornmeal

1 clove garlic, minced

1 tablespoon chopped fresh mint *or* 1 teaspoon crumbled dried mint

½ teaspoon salt

¼ teaspoon ground cumin

Dash black pepper

6 cups water

3 cans (10½ ounces each) condensed beef broth, undiluted

1 onion, chopped

¼ cup sliced celery

1 carrot, chopped

1 zucchini, chopped

1 yellow squash, chopped

½ bunch spinach, stemmed and cut into ½-inch strips

2 limes, cut into wedges

1. Combine beef, eggs, cornmeal, garlic, mint, salt, cumin and pepper in medium bowl. Shape mixture into 1-inch balls; set aside.

2. Combine water, broth, onion and celery in large saucepan or Dutch oven; bring to a boil over high heat. Reduce heat to low; simmer 10 minutes.

3. Add meatballs; simmer 5 minutes. Skim fat and foam from surface of broth. Add carrot, zucchini and yellow squash; simmer 20 minutes or until vegetables are tender.

4. Add spinach; simmer 5 minutes. Serve with lime wedges.   *Makes 6 servings*

albondigas soup

middle eastern chicken soup

2½ **cups water**

1 **can (about 14 ounces) reduced-sodium chicken broth**

1 **can (about 15 ounces) chickpeas, rinsed and drained**

1 **cup chopped cooked chicken**

1 **small onion, chopped**

1 **carrot, chopped**

1 **clove garlic, minced**

1 **teaspoon dried oregano**

1 **teaspoon ground cumin**

½ **(10-ounce) package fresh spinach, stemmed and coarsely chopped**

⅛ **teaspoon black pepper**

1. Combine water, broth, chickpeas, chicken, onion, carrot, garlic, oregano and cumin in medium saucepan. Bring to a boil over high heat. Reduce heat to low; cover and simmer 15 minutes.

2. Stir in spinach and pepper; simmer, uncovered, 2 minutes or until wilted.

Makes 4 servings

mediterranean bean and sausage soup

½ **pound sweet or hot Italian pork sausage, casing removed**

2 **large onions, chopped (about 2 cups)**

4 **cups PREGO® Traditional Italian Sauce**

2 **cans (14 ounces each) SWANSON® Chicken Broth (Regular, Natural Goodness® or Certified Organic) (3½ cups)**

2 **cans (about 15 ounces each) black or pinto beans, rinsed and drained**

2 **cans (about 15 ounces each) white kidney (cannellini) beans or red kidney beans, rinsed and drained**

1. Cook the sausage and onions in a 3-quart saucepan over medium-high heat until the sausage is well browned, stirring frequently to break up meat. Pour off any fat.

2. Stir the sauce and broth into the saucepan. Heat to a boil. Reduce the heat to low. Cook for 10 minutes. Add the beans. Heat, stirring occasionally, until hot.

Makes 8 servings

Prep Time: 10 minutes
Cook Time: 25 minutes

spicy thai shrimp soup

    1 tablespoon vegetable oil

    1 pound medium raw shrimp, peeled, shells reserved

    1 jalapeño pepper,* cut into slivers

    1 tablespoon paprika

  ¼ teaspoon ground red pepper

    4 cans (about 14 ounces each) reduced-sodium chicken broth

    1 (½-inch) strip *each* lemon and lime peel

    1 can (15 ounces) straw mushrooms, drained

      Juice of 1 lemon

      Juice of 1 lime

    2 tablespoons reduced-sodium soy sauce

    1 red Thai pepper,* red jalapeño pepper* *or* ¼ small red bell pepper, cut into strips

  ¼ cup fresh cilantro leaves

Chile peppers can sting and irritate the skin, so wear rubber gloves when handling peppers and do not touch your eyes.

1. Heat oil in large saucepan or wok over medium-high heat. Add shrimp, jalapeño, paprika and ground red pepper; cook and stir 2 minutes or until shrimp are pink and opaque. Remove from saucepan; set aside.

2. Add shrimp shells to saucepan; cook and stir 30 seconds. Add broth and lemon and lime peels; bring to a boil. Reduce heat to low; cover and simmer 15 minutes.

3. Remove shells and peels with slotted spoon; discard. Add mushrooms and shrimp mixture to broth; bring to a boil. Stir in lemon and lime juices, soy sauce and Thai pepper. Sprinkle each serving with cilantro. Serve immediately.   *Makes 8 servings*

spicy thai shrimp soup

slow cooker

pumpkin soup with bacon and toasted pumpkin seeds

  2 **teaspoons olive oil**
½ **cup raw pumpkin seeds**
  1 **medium onion, chopped**
  1 **teaspoon kosher salt**
½ **teaspoon chopped dried chipotle pepper**
½ **teaspoon black pepper**
  2 **cans (29 ounces each) solid-pack pumpkin**
  4 **cups chicken stock or broth**
¾ **cup apple cider**
½ **cup whipping cream**
    Sour cream
  3 **slices thick-sliced bacon, crisp-cooked and crumbled**

Slow Cooker Directions

1. Heat oil in medium skillet over medium heat. Add pumpkin seeds; cook and stir 1 minute or until seeds begin to pop. Transfer to small bowl; set aside.

2. Add onion to skillet; cook and stir over medium heat 5 minutes or until translucent. Stir in salt, chipotle pepper and black pepper. Transfer to slow cooker. Whisk in pumpkin, stock and apple cider; stir until smooth. Cover; cook on HIGH 4 hours.

3. Turn off slow cooker. Whisk in whipping cream. Season to taste with additional salt and pepper. Strain soup; garnish with sour cream, toasted pumpkin seeds and bacon.

Makes 4 to 6 servings

pumpkin soup with bacon
and toasted pumpkin seeds

moroccan chicken soup

4 cups SWANSON® Chicken Broth (Regular, Natural Goodness® or Certified Organic)

3 cloves garlic, minced

2 tablespoons honey

2 teaspoons ground cumin

½ teaspoon ground cinnamon

1 can (about 14½ ounces) diced tomatoes, undrained

1 large green pepper, cut into 2-inch-long strips (about 2 cups)

1 medium onion, chopped (1 cup)

½ cup raisins

8 skinless, boneless chicken thighs (about 1 pound), cut up

Hot cooked orzo (optional)

Slow Cooker Directions

1. Stir the broth, garlic, honey, cumin, cinnamon, tomatoes, green pepper, onion and raisins in a 3½- to 6-quart slow cooker. Add the chicken.

2. Cover and cook on LOW for 8 hours* or until the chicken is cooked through.

3. Divide the soup among **4** serving bowls. Place about **½ cup** orzo centered on top of **each** of the serving bowls. *Makes 4 servings*

*Or on HIGH for 4 hours

Prep Time: 10 minutes
Cook Time: 8 hours

moroccan chicken soup

creamy cauliflower bisque

1 pound frozen cauliflower florets, thawed

1 pound russet potatoes, peeled and cut into 1-inch cubes

1 cup chopped onion

½ teaspoon dried thyme

¼ teaspoon garlic powder

⅛ teaspoon ground red pepper

2 cans (about 14 ounces each) reduced-sodium vegetable or chicken broth

1 cup evaporated milk

2 tablespoons butter

½ teaspoon salt

¼ teaspoon black pepper

1 cup (4 ounces) shredded sharp Cheddar cheese

¼ cup finely chopped fresh parsley

¼ cup finely chopped green onions

Slow Cooker Directions

1. Layer cauliflower, potatoes, onion, thyme, garlic powder and red pepper in slow cooker. Pour in broth. Cover; cook on LOW 8 hours or on HIGH 4 hours.

2. Process soup in batches in food processor or blender until smooth; return to slow cooker. Add evaporated milk, butter, salt and black pepper. Cook, uncovered, on HIGH 30 minutes or until heated through.

3. Top each serving with cheese, parsley and green onions.   *Makes 8 servings*

creamy cauliflower bisque

nancy's chicken noodle soup

2 boneless skinless chicken breasts, cut into bite-size pieces

⅔ cup diced onion

⅔ cup diced celery

⅔ cup diced carrots

⅔ cup sliced mushrooms

½ cup frozen peas

2 tablespoons butter or margarine

4 chicken bouillon cubes

1 tablespoon dried parsley flakes

1 teaspoon salt

1 teaspoon ground cumin

1 teaspoon dried marjoram

1 teaspoon black pepper

1 can (about 48 ounces) chicken broth

4 cups water

2 cups cooked egg noodles

Slow Cooker Directions

1. Combine chicken, onion, celery, carrots, mushrooms, peas, butter, bouillon cubes, parsley flakes, salt, cumin, marjoram and pepper in slow cooker. Pour in broth and water.

2. Cover; cook on LOW 5 to 7 hours or on HIGH 3 to 4 hours. Stir in noodles 30 minutes before serving.

Makes 8 servings

nancy's chicken noodle soup

potato & spinach soup with gouda

6 cups cubed peeled Yukon Gold potatoes (about 9 medium)

2 cans (about 14 ounces each) vegetable or chicken broth

½ cup water

1 small red onion, finely chopped

5 ounces baby spinach

½ teaspoon salt

¼ teaspoon ground red pepper

¼ teaspoon black pepper

2½ cups shredded smoked Gouda cheese, divided

1 can (12 ounces) evaporated milk

1 tablespoon olive oil

4 cloves garlic, cut into thin slices

Chopped fresh parsley

Slow Cooker Directions

1. Combine potatoes, broth, water, onion, spinach, salt, red pepper and black pepper in slow cooker. Cover; cook on LOW 10 hours or on HIGH 4 to 5 hours.

2. *Turn slow cooker to HIGH.* Slightly mash potatoes in slow cooker; add 2 cups cheese and evaporated milk. Cover; cook on HIGH 15 to 20 minutes or until cheese is melted.

3. Heat oil in small skillet over low heat. Add garlic; cook and stir 2 minutes or until golden brown. Sprinkle soup with garlic, remaining ½ cup cheese and parsley.

Makes 8 to 10 servings

 Yukon Gold potatoes are thin-skinned, pale yellow-gold potatoes with pale yellow flesh. When buying potatoes, make sure there are no bruises, sprouts or green areas. Store Yukon Golds in a cool dark place and use within 1 week of purchase.

potato & spinach soup with gouda

hearty mushroom and barley soup

 9 cups vegetable or chicken broth

 1 package (16 ounces) sliced button mushrooms

 1 onion, chopped

 2 carrots, chopped

 2 stalks celery, chopped

 ½ cup uncooked pearl barley

 ½ ounce dried porcini mushrooms

 3 cloves garlic, minced

 1 teaspoon salt

 ½ teaspoon dried thyme

 ½ teaspoon black pepper

Slow Cooker Directions

Combine broth, button mushrooms, onion, carrots, celery, barley, porcini mushrooms, garlic, salt, thyme and pepper in slow cooker. Cover; cook on LOW 4 to 6 hours.

Makes 8 to 10 servings

Variation: For even more flavor, add a beef or ham bone to the slow cooker with the rest of the ingredients.

navy bean and ham soup

 6 cups water

 5 cups dried navy beans, soaked overnight, rinsed and drained

 1 pound ham, cubed

 1 can (about 15 ounces) whole kernel corn, drained

 1 can (4 ounces) mild diced green chiles, drained

 1 onion, diced

   Salt and black pepper

Slow Cooker Directions

Combine water, beans, ham, corn, chiles, onion, salt and pepper in slow cooker. Cover; cook on LOW 8 to 10 hours or until beans are softened.

Makes 6 servings

hearty mushroom and barley soup

simple turkey soup

2 pounds ground turkey, cooked and drained

1 can (28 ounces) whole tomatoes, undrained

2 cans (about 14 ounces each) beef broth

1 package (16 ounces) frozen mixed soup vegetables (such as carrots, beans, okra, corn or onion), thawed

½ cup uncooked barley

1 teaspoon salt

1 teaspoon dried thyme

½ teaspoon ground coriander

Black pepper

Slow Cooker Directions

Combine turkey, tomatoes, broth, vegetables, barley, salt, thyme, coriander and black pepper in slow cooker. Add water to cover. Cover; cook on HIGH 3 to 4 hours.

Makes 8 servings

 | Try adding other frozen or canned vegetables or extra diced potatoes and carrots to this soup. Sliced, diced or stewed tomatoes can be substituted for the whole tomatoes. For a large crowd, add corn and serve with corn bread.

simple turkey soup

classic french onion soup

¼ cup (½ stick) butter

3 large onions, sliced

1 cup dry white wine

3 cans (about 14 ounces each) beef or vegetable broth

1 teaspoon Worcestershire sauce

½ teaspoon salt

½ teaspoon dried thyme

4 slices French bread, toasted

1 cup (4 ounces) shredded Swiss cheese

Slow Cooker Directions

1. Melt butter in large skillet over medium heat. Add onions; cook and stir 15 minutes or until onions are soft and lightly browned. Stir in wine.

2. Combine onion mixture, broth, Worcestershire sauce, salt and thyme in slow cooker. Cover; cook on LOW 4 to 4½ hours.

3. Preheat broiler. Ladle soup into 4 ovenproof bowls; top with bread slice and cheese. Broil until cheese melts.   *Makes 4 servings*

slow cooker sausage vegetable soup

1 pound BOB EVANS® Original Recipe Sausage Roll

3 cans (14 ounces each) reduced sodium chicken broth

1 package (20 ounces) BOB EVANS® Home Fries diced potatoes

1 package (16 ounces) frozen mixed vegetables

1 can (8 ounces) tomato sauce

Slow Cooker Directions

In a medium skillet over medium heat, crumble and cook sausage until brown. Place in slow cooker. Add remaining ingredients. Cover and cook on LOW 6 to 8 hours.

Makes 8 servings

Prep Time: 10 minutes
Cook Time: 6 to 8 hours

classic french onion soup

beer and cheese soup

2 to 3 slices pumpernickel or rye bread

1 can (about 14 ounces) vegetable or chicken broth

1 cup beer

¼ cup finely chopped onion

2 cloves garlic, minced

¾ teaspoon dried thyme

1½ cups (6 ounces) shredded American cheese

1½ cups (6 ounces) shredded sharp Cheddar cheese

1 cup milk

½ teaspoon paprika

Slow Cooker Directions

1. For croutons, preheat oven to 425°F. Slice bread into ½-inch cubes; place on baking sheet. Bake 10 to 12 minutes or until crisp, stirring once; set aside.

2. Combine broth, beer, onion, garlic and thyme in slow cooker. Cover; cook on LOW 4 hours.

3. *Turn slow cooker to HIGH.* Stir in cheeses, milk and paprika. Cover; cook 1 hour or until heated through. Top with croutons.   *Makes 4 servings*

slow cooker chicken & wild rice soup

1 pound boneless, skinless chicken breasts, cubed

½ cup uncooked wild rice, rinsed thoroughly

2 medium carrots, peeled and shredded

2 stalks celery, thinly sliced

1 large yellow onion, chopped

5½ cups water

2 tablespoons HERB-OX® chicken flavored bouillon

1 cup heavy whipping cream

2 tablespoons all-purpose flour

Slivered almonds, for garnish

Slow Cooker Directions

In large (6-quart) slow cooker, combine all ingredients, with the exception of the heavy cream, flour and almond slivers. Cover and cook on the LOW heat setting for 4 hours or until the chicken is cooked through and the rice is tender. Just before serving, combine the heavy cream and the flour. Slowly stir the cream mixture into the soup. Cook and stir constantly for 5 minutes or until the mixture is slightly thickened. Ladle into bowls and garnish with slivered almonds. *Makes 6 to 8 servings*

beef, lentil and onion soup

1 tablespoon olive oil

¾ pound beef for stew (1-inch pieces)

2 cups chopped carrots

1 cup sliced celery

1 cup uncooked lentils

2 teaspoons dried thyme

¼ teaspoon black pepper

⅛ teaspoon salt

3¼ cups water

1 can (10¾ ounces) condensed French onion soup, undiluted

Slow Cooker Directions

1. Heat oil in large skillet over medium-high heat. Add beef; cook until browned on all sides.

2. Layer carrots, celery, lentils and beef in slow cooker. Sprinkle with thyme, pepper and salt. Pour water and soup into slow cooker.

3. Cover; cook on LOW 7 to 8 hours or on HIGH 3½ to 4 hours or until meat and lentils are tender. *Makes 6 servings*

sweet and sour cabbage soup

2 pounds boneless beef chuck roast

1 can (about 28 ounces) whole tomatoes, cut into pieces, undrained

1 can (15 ounces) tomato sauce

1 large onion, thinly sliced

3 carrots, shredded

2 pounds green cabbage, shredded

4 cups water

¾ cup sugar

½ cup lemon juice

1 tablespoon caraway seeds

2 teaspoons salt

1 teaspoon black pepper

Slow Cooker Directions

1. Cut beef into 4 pieces. Spray large skillet with nonstick cooking spray; heat over medium-high heat. Brown meat on all sides; transfer to slow cooker. Add tomatoes, tomato sauce, onion, carrots, cabbage, water, sugar, lemon juice, caraway seeds, salt and pepper. Cover; cook on LOW 6 to 8 hours.

2. Remove beef from slow cooker. Shred beef and return to slow cooker; heat through.

Makes 8 to 10 servings

sweet and sour cabbage soup

thai coconut chicken and rice soup

1 pound boneless skinless chicken thighs, cut into 1-inch pieces

3 cups reduced-sodium chicken broth

1 package (12 ounces) frozen chopped onions

1 can (4 ounces) sliced mushrooms, drained

2 tablespoons minced fresh ginger

2 tablespoons sugar

1 can (14 ounces) unsweetened coconut milk

1 cup cooked rice

½ red bell pepper, seeded and thinly sliced

3 tablespoons chopped fresh cilantro

2 tablespoons grated lime peel

Slow Cooker Directions

1. Combine chicken, broth, onions, mushrooms, ginger and sugar in slow cooker. Cover; cook on LOW 8 to 9 hours.

2. Stir coconut milk, rice and bell pepper into soup. Cover; cook 15 minutes. Turn off heat; stir in cilantro and lime peel. *Makes 6 to 8 servings*

 Tip | One medium lime will yield about 1½ teaspoons grated lime peel. You will need about 4 medium limes to get 2 tablespoons grated lime peel.

thai coconut chicken and rice soup

italian sausage soup

Meatballs

    1 pound mild Italian sausage, casings removed

    ½ cup plain dry bread crumbs

    ¼ cup grated Parmesan cheese

    ¼ cup milk

    1 egg

    ½ teaspoon dried basil

    ½ teaspoon black pepper

    ¼ teaspoon garlic salt

Soup

    4 cups chicken broth

    1 tablespoon tomato paste

    1 clove garlic, minced

    ¼ teaspoon red pepper flakes

    ½ cup uncooked miniature shell pasta*

    1 package (10 ounces) baby spinach

    Additional grated Parmesan cheese (optional)

Or use other tiny pasta, such as ditalini (mini tubes) or farfallini (mini bowties).

Slow Cooker Directions

1. Combine all meatball ingredients in large bowl. Shape into ½-inch balls.

2. Combine broth, tomato paste, garlic and red pepper flakes in slow cooker. Add meatballs. Cover; cook on LOW 5 to 6 hours.

3. Add pasta; cook 30 minutes or until pasta is tender. Stir in spinach. Sprinkle with additional cheese, if desired. Serve immediately.   *Makes 4 to 6 servings*

italian sausage soup

potato and leek soup

    4 **cups chicken broth**

    3 **potatoes, peeled and diced**

1½ **cups chopped cabbage**

    1 **leek, diced**

    1 **onion, chopped**

    2 **carrots, diced**

  ¼ **cup chopped fresh parsley**

    1 **teaspoon salt**

  ½ **teaspoon caraway seeds**

  ½ **teaspoon black pepper**

    1 **bay leaf**

  ½ **cup sour cream**

    1 **pound bacon, cooked and crumbled**

Slow Cooker Directions

1. Combine broth, potatoes, cabbage, leek, onion, carrots, parsley, salt, caraway seeds, pepper and bay leaf in slow cooker; mix well.

2. Cover; cook on LOW 8 to 10 hours or on HIGH 4 to 5 hours.

3. Remove and discard bay leaf. Stir ½ cup hot liquid from slow cooker into sour cream in small bowl until smooth. Stir sour cream mixture and bacon into soup.

Makes 6 to 8 servings

potato and leek soup

hamburger soup

1 pound ground beef
1 cup thinly sliced carrots
1 cup sliced celery
1 package (1 ounce) dry onion soup mix
1 package (1 ounce) Italian salad dressing mix
¼ teaspoon seasoned salt
¼ teaspoon black pepper
3 cups boiling water
1 can (about 14 ounces) diced tomatoes
1 can (8 ounces) tomato sauce
1 tablespoon soy sauce
2 cups cooked macaroni
¼ cup grated Parmesan cheese
2 tablespoons chopped fresh parsley

Slow Cooker Directions

1. Brown ground beef in large skillet over medium-high heat 6 to 8 minutes, stirring to break up meat. Drain fat.

2. Place carrots and celery in slow cooker. Top with beef, soup mix, salad dressing mix, seasoned salt and pepper. Add water, tomatoes, tomato sauce and soy sauce; mix well. Cover; cook on LOW 6 to 8 hours.

3. *Turn slow cooker to HIGH.* Stir in macaroni and Parmesan cheese. Cover; cook 15 to 30 minutes or until heated through. Sprinkle with parsley just before serving.

Makes 6 to 8 servings

hamburger soup

slow-simmered chicken rice soup

½ **cup uncooked wild rice**

½ **cup uncooked regular long-grain white rice**

1 **tablespoon vegetable oil**

5¼ **cups SWANSON® Chicken Broth (Regular, Natural Goodness® or Certified Organic)**

2 **teaspoons dried thyme leaves, crushed**

¼ **teaspoon crushed red pepper**

2 **stalks celery, coarsely chopped (about 1 cup)**

1 **medium onion, chopped (about ½ cup)**

1 **pound skinless, boneless chicken breasts, cut into cubes**

Sour cream (optional)

Chopped green onions (optional)

Slow Cooker Directions

1. Stir the wild rice, white rice and oil in a 3½-quart slow cooker. Cover and cook on HIGH for 15 minutes.

2. Stir the broth, thyme, red pepper, celery, onion and chicken into the slow cooker. Turn the heat to LOW. Cover and cook on LOW for 7 to 8 hours* or until the chicken is cooked through.

3. Serve with the sour cream and green onions, if desired.   *Makes 8 servings*

*Or on HIGH for 4 to 5 hours

Time-Saving Tip: Speed preparation by substituting 3 cans (4.5 ounces each) SWANSON® Premium Chunk Chicken Breast, drained, for the raw chicken.

Prep Time: 15 minutes
Cook Time: 7 to 8 hours (LOW) • 4 to 5 hours (HIGH)

slow-simmered chicken rice soup

double corn chowder

1 cup corn

1 cup canned hominy

6 ounces Canadian bacon, chopped

2 stalks celery, chopped

1 small onion or large shallot, chopped

1 jalapeño pepper,* seeded and minced

¼ teaspoon salt

¼ teaspoon dried thyme

¼ teaspoon black pepper

1 cup chicken broth

1½ cups milk,** divided

1 tablespoon all-purpose flour

*Jalapeño peppers can sting and irritate the skin, so wear rubber gloves when handling peppers and do not touch your eyes.

**For richer chowder, use ¾ cup milk and ¾ cup half-and-half.

Slow Cooker Directions

1. Combine corn, hominy, bacon, celery, onion, jalapeño, salt, thyme and black pepper in slow cooker. Add broth. Cover; cook on LOW 5 to 6 hours or on HIGH 3 to 3½ hours.

2. Whisk 2 tablespoons milk into flour in small bowl until smooth. Stir into slow cooker. Add remaining milk. Cover; cook on LOW 20 minutes or until slightly thickened and heated through.   *Makes 4 servings*

double corn chowder

tuscan white bean soup

    6 ounces bacon, diced
   10 cups chicken broth
    1 package (16 ounces) dried Great Northern beans, rinsed and sorted
    1 can (about 14 ounces) diced tomatoes
    1 large onion, chopped
    3 carrots, chopped
    4 cloves garlic, minced
    1 fresh rosemary sprig *or* 1 teaspoon dried rosemary
    1 teaspoon black pepper

Slow Cooker Directions

1. Cook bacon in medium skillet over medium heat until crisp; drain on paper towels. Transfer to slow cooker. Add broth, beans, tomatoes, onion, carrots, garlic, rosemary and pepper.

2. Cover; cook on LOW 8 hours or until beans are tender. Remove and discard rosemary before serving.   *Makes 8 to 10 servings*

Serving Suggestion: Place slices of toasted Italian bread in bottom of individual soup bowls. Drizzle with olive oil. Ladle soup over bread.

butternut squash-apple soup

    3 packages (12 ounces each) frozen cooked winter squash, thawed and drained
        or about 4½ cups mashed cooked butternut squash
    2 cans (about 14 ounces each) vegetable broth
    1 medium Golden Delicious apple, peeled and chopped
    2 tablespoons minced onion
    1 tablespoon packed brown sugar
    1 teaspoon minced fresh sage *or* ½ teaspoon ground sage
   ¼ teaspoon ground ginger
   ½ cup whipping cream or half-and-half

Slow Cooker Directions

1. Combine squash, broth, apple, onion, brown sugar, sage and ginger in slow cooker.

2. Cover; cook on LOW 6 hours or on HIGH 3 hours.

3. Process soup in batches in food processor or blender until smooth. Return to slow cooker. Stir in cream just before serving.   *Makes 6 to 8 servings*

tuscan white bean soup

roasted tomato-basil soup

    2 cans (28 ounces each) whole tomatoes, drained and juice reserved

    1 onion, finely chopped

2½ tablespoons packed dark brown sugar

    3 cups vegetable or chicken broth

    3 tablespoons tomato paste

    ¼ teaspoon ground allspice

    1 can (5 ounces) evaporated milk

    ¼ cup chopped fresh basil

    Salt and black pepper

    Additional fresh basil (optional)

Slow Cooker Directions

1. Preheat oven to 450°F. Line baking sheet with foil; spray with nonstick cooking spray. Arrange tomatoes on foil in single layer. Sprinkle with onion and brown sugar. Bake 25 to 30 minutes or until tomatoes look dry and are lightly browned. Let tomatoes cool slightly; finely chop.

2. Place tomato mixture, reserved tomato juice, broth, tomato paste and allspice in slow cooker; mix well. Cover; cook on LOW 8 hours or on HIGH 4 hours.

3. Add evaporated milk and basil; season with salt and pepper. Cook on HIGH 30 minutes or until heated through. Garnish with fresh basil.   *Makes 6 servings*

acknowledgments

The publisher would like to thank the companies and organizations listed below for the use of their recipes and photographs in this publication.

The Beef Checkoff

Bob Evans®

Campbell Soup Company

ConAgra Foods, Inc.

Del Monte Foods

Dole Food Company, Inc.

Filippo Berio® Olive Oil

Hormel Foods, LLC

Jennie-O Turkey Store, LLC

Kraft Foods Global, Inc.

McIlhenny Company (TABASCO® brand Pepper Sauce)

Michael Foods, Inc.

National Fisheries Institute

National Pork Board

National Turkey Federation

Ortega®, A Division of B&G Foods, Inc.

Reckitt Benckiser Inc.

StarKist®

Tyson Foods, Inc.

Unilever

metric conversion chart

VOLUME MEASUREMENTS (dry)

$^1/_8$ teaspoon = 0.5 mL
$^1/_4$ teaspoon = 1 mL
$^1/_2$ teaspoon = 2 mL
$^3/_4$ teaspoon = 4 mL
1 teaspoon = 5 mL
1 tablespoon = 15 mL
2 tablespoons = 30 mL
$^1/_4$ cup = 60 mL
$^1/_3$ cup = 75 mL
$^1/_2$ cup = 125 mL
$^2/_3$ cup = 150 mL
$^3/_4$ cup = 175 mL
1 cup = 250 mL
2 cups = 1 pint = 500 mL
3 cups = 750 mL
4 cups = 1 quart = 1 L

VOLUME MEASUREMENTS (fluid)

1 fluid ounce (2 tablespoons) = 30 mL
4 fluid ounces ($^1/_2$ cup) = 125 mL
8 fluid ounces (1 cup) = 250 mL
12 fluid ounces (1$^1/_2$ cups) = 375 mL
16 fluid ounces (2 cups) = 500 mL

WEIGHTS (mass)

$^1/_2$ ounce = 15 g
1 ounce = 30 g
3 ounces = 90 g
4 ounces = 120 g
8 ounces = 225 g
10 ounces = 285 g
12 ounces = 360 g
16 ounces = 1 pound = 450 g

DIMENSIONS

$^1/_{16}$ inch = 2 mm
$^1/_8$ inch = 3 mm
$^1/_4$ inch = 6 mm
$^1/_2$ inch = 1.5 cm
$^3/_4$ inch = 2 cm
1 inch = 2.5 cm

OVEN TEMPERATURES

250°F = 120°C
275°F = 140°C
300°F = 150°C
325°F = 160°C
350°F = 180°C
375°F = 190°C
400°F = 200°C
425°F = 220°C
450°F = 230°C

BAKING PAN SIZES

Utensil	Size in Inches/Quarts	Metric Volume	Size in Centimeters
Baking or Cake Pan (square or rectangular)	8×8×2	2 L	20×20×5
	9×9×2	2.5 L	23×23×5
	12×8×2	3 L	30×20×5
	13×9×2	3.5 L	33×23×5
Loaf Pan	8×4×3	1.5 L	20×10×7
	9×5×3	2 L	23×13×7
Round Layer Cake Pan	8×1½	1.2 L	20×4
	9×1½	1.5 L	23×4
Pie Plate	8×1¼	750 mL	20×3
	9×1¼	1 L	23×3
Baking Dish or Casserole	1 quart	1 L	—
	1½ quart	1.5 L	—
	2 quart	2 L	—